Lovers of life, these two sisters wish to share with you a different perspective on life.

They call these 'whispers of the universe' that will beckon you to re-look at your life and wonder – is life just our perception based on our experiences and assumptions or is there more to it?

Dedication

We dedicate this book to
you,
for your effort to understand life and your existence.

We also dedicate this book to our loving parents,
Uma and Raj,
for being our inspiration throughout our lives.

We, sisters, would also like to dedicate this book to each other, as it has taught us to appreciate and love life more than we did before. The words in this book have inspired and motivated us to continue moving ahead with joy within, irrespective of the challenges that life brought our way.

Palak and Pooja

IS LIFE AS WE KNOW IT?

AUSTIN MACAULEY PUBLISHERS™

LONDON • CAMBRIDGE • NEW YORK • SHARJAH

ISBN 9789948390534 (Paperback)
ISBN 9789948390527 (E-Book)

Application Number: MC-02-01-5742741
Age Classification: E

The age group that matches the content of the books has been classified according to the age classification system issued by the National Media Council.

Printer Name: iPrint Global Ltd.
Printer Address: Witchford, England.

First Published (2019)
AUSTIN MACAULEY PUBLISHERS FZE
Sharjah Publishing City
P.O Box [519201]
Sharjah, UAE
www.austinmacauley.ae
+971 655 95 202

Acknowledgements

We feel blessed and are very grateful to our family members and friends for their love, endless support and encouragement.

Thanks to our parents and our respective spouses for patiently listening to our work and offering valuable feedback.

Thank you Kashish, Saif, Jiya and Samir, our beautiful children, for being our inspiration and for holding our hands while providing guidance during this beautiful journey.

We are very grateful to our dearest friend Ritu Kartha who has been an integral part of this book and our lives.

We are also deeply grateful to have each other as sisters in this life as we continue this journey of learning and experience unconditional love, support, allowance and so much more, together.

Further, we take this opportunity to thank the following people who have played a key role in our lives, and during this book's journey:

Pooja: Nilofer Safder and Ritu Motial, thank you for teaching me that life is filled with possibilities.

Palak: Fauzia Ansari who is responsible for starting my romance with reading and writing when I was in high school.

Also Reyna Rupani, the creator of a ladies writing group where I got an opportunity to sharpen my writing skills and experience being a journalist.

We are also indebted to the following authors and well-known people who have influenced us in this journey:

Swami Vivekananda, Paramhansa Yogananda, Dr Wayne W. Dyer, Esther and Jerry Hicks, Sadhguru, Oprah Winfrey, Gary Douglas, Dr Dain Heer, Simone Milasas, Glenyce Hughes, Mike Dooley, Robin Sharma, Rhonda Byrne, Jake Ducey and many more. These names are in random order.

Table of Contents

Choices   177

Introduction

We are so excited that you chose to read this book. We hope that it offers you a new perspective on life and our existence. It sure has changed ours, and we are more in love with life now than we were ever before. It has left us wanting to live every moment consciously with joy and passion.

We, two sisters, are eager to share this book with you – a book that is a compilation of beautiful and thoughtful information that will beckon you to relook at life and wonder, is life really as we know it?

Our writing journey started in our childhood, in diaries and letters that we used to write to each other. This book, however, started suddenly, one day in 2017.

Pooja: "Palak, you cannot imagine what I wrote! Stop whatever you are doing and listen."

Palak: "What? What did you write?"

Pooja: "In life, there are two kinds of people. Some people are *achche* (a Hindi word for good or nice) and then there are those who are *sachche* (a Hindi word for truthful)."

Palak: "Oh my God! That explains it!"

Pooja: "Huh? Explains what?"

Palak: "This is the answer to something that I have been contemplating for the past couple of days."

Pooja: "You were? What is it?"

Palak: "I have always believed that every human being has goodness within. One judges a person to be good or bad depending upon one's experiences with that person. If the encounter is favourable, then that person is good; if not, then that person is labelled as not-so-nice. However, Pooja, this has taken it one step further. Even that so-called not nice is not negative at all. That person is just being true to himself – to whatever he or she is going through and experiencing, which is flavoured with his conditioning and beliefs."

We discussed this for hours that night and we saw so much of truth in it.

Palak: "What made you write this?"
Pooja: "I don't know. I just had a strong urge to write and immediately wanted to share it with you."

This is how our journey of writing began in 2017. The contents of this book were first written by Pooja. Whenever she had an urge to write, she would grab whatever paper she could lay her hands on, write it down and then called me immediately. I remember being awed each time she called. We would end up discussing her writing for hours. We could relate to these words easily and found solace in them. It made us wonder, is life really as we know it?

We started sharing these with our close friends who would many times gift us with a completely different perspective. This is the beauty of the information that you are about to read. We soon decided to compile these into a book.

Here is a little bit about us, the authors.

Palak: "Writing has always helped me express my thoughts, emotions and feelings. As cliché as it may sound, I have always found that writing gave me clarity.

I clearly remember, in 1984, when I was still in school, I had read a chapter called 'Habit of Reading', written by Dr S. Radhakrishnan. I was so impressed by his writing that I had written down my feelings on a square piece of paper, expressing my wish to become a philosopher one day. I still have that paper.

However, at the time of selecting a subject to major in, for my graduation, I was aiming for English. Imagine my amazement at the well-designed scheme of the universe that I was accepted into a college of my choice and was offered Philosophy as my main subject. I was ridiculed then by a few, that Philosophy was opted by losers, those who didn't get accepted in subjects of their choice. Soon, my fascination for this subject took over and I found myself opening up to new possibilities, ideas and realising that various schools of thoughts, however contrary they may seem, could co-exist. It expanded my thinking and I believe that it was the foundation for things that were to come later in my life. It helped me question and understand life and our existence.

While growing up, I harboured a desire to write books. I remember, many years ago, I had declared to some colleagues that I was writing a book. When asked 'What are you writing about?' I had mumbled 'my experiences (what my life had taught me)', while my mind was saying 'who cares about your experiences in the larger scheme of life?' Hence, my writings stuck to 'Dear Diary' and 'Hello God'."

Pooja: "Oh yes, I remember. I used to guard your dairies when you were away from home."

Palak: "I had forgotten about that. Well, as time passed by, I graduated from diaries to a computer which was a gift from my husband, and that's when my love for writing went to a whole new level. I became a member of a ladies writing group and started writing for the local newspapers and magazines as a freelance writer.

In 2000, my dream of becoming an author came to a standstill as I had decided to join the corporate world and take up a full-time job. There, I came across many beautiful people from different parts of the globe and learned so much from each one of them.

Then in 2016 came 'the day' – the day I chose to quit my job and focus on being at home with my daughter who was experiencing a health challenge. Little did I know that my new lifestyle was a perfect setting for me to begin writing again. My sister started reminding me to write my book, but I was not sure of what to write. Besides, who would want to hear what I have to say? I started looking for some guidance, some inspiration to write. I wanted to write passionately but didn't know where to start.

Meanwhile, staying at home, I found myself getting fascinated by Dr Wayne W. Dyer's books. I loved the ease with which he wrote and spoke. Subjects on Mysticism and Spirituality fascinated me. I continued reading, listening and was introduced to the work done by authors such as Swami Vivekananda and Paramhansa Yogananda – Autobiography of a Yogi, which was a book gifted to me by you, Pooja.

This is when we both read a lot of books. This was our new-found passion, and we sisters would discuss various schools of thoughts for hours each day. Then one day, Pooja called me and said that the previous night, she had experienced an unusual urge to write."

Pooja: "Yes, I tried to ignore it many times as I was listening to Esther Hicks-Abraham online, but it just wouldn't go away. Eventually, I did give in. I picked up a pen and began writing, and boy did I write! Words just kept pouring out and I was on a roll. Thus began our journey – a journey of mesmerising words that exuded awe and strength.

At first, these were random words that made no sense, but soon, beautiful words started to flow with ease. It was as if I had connected to a reservoir of knowledge, and information just flowed in. Excitedly, I began sharing these with Palak, and together we would marvel at their simplicity and beauty. Relating to many, we would discuss them for hours, citing simple examples from our daily lives. This had become a daily ritual. We decided to compile these messages into a book and thus began our journey of writing.

I started writing at a very young age when Palak had left home for higher studies. When she was home, I used to share all my feelings with her on a daily basis. So, when she left home, I would end up writing letters to her, as I had to let her know what I did each day. However, there were times when I would spend nights writing to God, asking questions, waiting for answers, as there were so many things that I was a witness to, that I didn't understand and didn't quite get. Writing was never my passion, communicating with my sister and writing to God was. Writing as such was not my passion, it was yours, Palak."

Palak: "I used to love your letters, Pooja. They were full of life and I used to read them over and over again. It's more than 20 years now that we are living in the same city and not a day goes by when we have not spoken to each other."

We are so happy to share these writings with you in the form of this book. So, sit back and marvel at the beauty of these messages and how they whisper the secrets of the universe.

No matter where you are at present in your life – high in happiness, nothing much happening or beneath a boulder of stress, sadness or pain – you will find some messages in this book that will make you think and re-examine your beliefs. They will offer you a new perspective and a strange sort of comfort and peace within.

The topics in this book range from questions that will leave you introspecting, to ones that will make you re-evaluate everything that you thought, you knew.

Is life really as we know it?

LIFE

1. Is Life a Thrilling Experience?

In this reality, some things are very clear. When you give people a task to finish, how would you encourage them to finish it? You would find a stimulus to encourage them, isn't it? Similarly, in order to achieve a goal, a task or a life purpose, there are some stimuli put forth by the Universe that help us.

Imagine: just dropping here on earth and experiencing things without any sense of achievement or adventure. How boring is that! Mundane, ordinary and nothing to excite us. What is the point of coming into this reality, then? With just the usual boring routine stuff, we would soon be depressed, isn't it?

Imagine a life that is plain, as plain as a straight line.

Is this interesting? Will this be a reason for you to choose to come down to earth, for just a straight line?

Now, look at this…

/\/

That's life! That is what shows *'life is'* on the heart monitors in the hospitals. And what does a straight line ______________________________ signify on the same monitor?

/\/\/\/\/\/\/\/\/\/\/\/\ This is life.

___________________________ This is not life.

Experience creates /\/\/\/\/\/\/\/\/\/\.

Experiencing the journey, where stimuli is presented by the universe is /\/\/\/\/\/\/\/\/\/\ a.k.a. life.

_________________________________ This is no creation. It is a soul-less body.

So, what is life and what are we?

Just relax. All will be _________________________________ eventually, anyway. What is the point of living in doubt or fear? Right now, let us enjoy and experience this life.

To know life, we need to experience it first, isn't it? Live it to know it.

/\/\/\/\/\/\/\/\/\/\ i.e. LIFE.

Imagine a surfer on the beach. The waves come and go, continuously. Some waves are strong, big and challenging whereas some are small, gentle and are easily managed by the surfer. All the surfer does is try to balance himself on the surfboard amidst waves that swell and fall. He seeks his thrill by staying on the surfboard.

Does he go out surfing when the waves are not strong, and the sea is calm? No. There is no upliftment then, no thrill and no experience. He enjoys and is thrilled only when he experiences and conquers the waves. If he falls, he gets up again and continues surfing. This is what life on earth is all about.

Perhaps life is an adventure that we experience while we try to maintain our balance as we surf across waves that are often challenging. The adventurous ride is what makes life worthwhile, isn't it?

2. Is Future a Mystery?

Why do you want to know your future?

The essence of life is in searching, looking, finding, learning, and then creating a conclusion, then further evolving.

Why do you want to know everything ahead of time? What's the fun, then? Where is the essence of life here? How will you learn?

How will you create your story, your journey, your excitement if you know your future?

Your future has endless possibilities and you will shape your future based on the options that you choose.

Trust your knowing. The whole universe is watching you and is with you!

3. I Don't Know

Life, as we see and know it, is influenced by one's past. There are no 'ifs' and 'buts' about it. Past experiences, conditioning, thoughts, beliefs, etc. are influencers. However, it is only through new experiences, meeting new people, reading new books, experiencing new age thoughts and mingling with the new generation that one can experiment with new ways, learn and move forward.

Let us try an experiment. Call someone 'new' or something 'new' into your existence. Imagine something that is 'beyond your imagination'. Can you? No. It is not possible!

Now try to imagine a new colour. Can you? You will keep seeing colours that you have already seen. So, can you imagine a new colour? No.

First, let us get this. Whatever one imagines or believes in, is from a limited space, isn't it? That's because we are souls or spirits living in a finite body that occupies limited space. To go beyond one's limited space, one has to go to the space that is 'beyond one's imagination'. Now, that space does exist, but humankind is not there, yet. Our brains are not that evolved yet.

We run our world based on our perception, experiences, assumption and imagination.

Our perception of life is based on:
- our past and present experiences that enable us to understand life;
- other's past and present experiences that make us aware of possibilities;
- our imagination of the future that takes us to another level of life altogether.

But our 'imagination' is also influenced by others' and our past and present experiences, isn't it? Now, these experiences create our thought process. Moreover, to what extent we push our thoughts, creates a 'new connection in our brain' that leads to the imagination of an enhanced future.

So, how do we go beyond that space? We can never be a hundred percent sure that 'something is a fact' unless we have experienced it ourselves, isn't it?

So, what is required to go beyond?

It is the zest to live; the enthusiasm within; the desire to create 'beyond what we know'; and to believe that there is always something else possible. To be able to go to that space of 'what-if' and trust that there can be another possibility and another simple way. Then we can say, *'I am aware of the space that exists beyond my imagination and I am aware that something beyond my knowledge can also exist.'*

So we don't know what is happening and going on here, in this chaos, isn't it? 'Don't know' are magical words. Let us be in the space of 'I don't know'. Isn't this a wow space to be in? It is a space where there is nothing to fight for, nor against. It is a peaceful space to be in.

Since we all live in a finite body in our limited space, we actually have limited knowledge.

'Don't know' is better than an assumption leading to a belief and then to war.

'Don't know' is simple.

'Don't know' – *'You can argue as much as you want, but I don't know so I will choose to keep quiet.'*

'Don't know' doesn't mean that one is putting oneself down. It simply means that I don't know! Just as *'I don't know French because I have never learned it'* or *'I don't know Japanese as I have not learned it. It does not make me less smart.'*

Our life as we know it, is 'as we know it'. Let's go into the space of 'don't know it' – the space that is beyond our imagination. 'I don't know' opens up a whole new universe of possibilities.

For if we say that we know it all, it is a kind of a limitation, isn't it? It is as if there is no space in our cup for more, as it is already full of 'what we know'. There is so much that we don't know and there is always a scope of knowing more, isn't it? So, is life really as we know it?

Don't know is like a fresh start.
It is similar to starting from zero again
and that opens up to infinite possibilities.

4. Asking with Doubt?
Don't Bother, It Will Not Happen

This is a very good time for you to understand and realise that life is fruitful if you are removed out of the equation. Why? That's because you bring in doubt, and 'asking with doubt' is not asking.

Asking with affirmation, asking with belief and knowing, asking with a smile and a twinkle in your eye, will make it happen. That's because 'you' have asked, and 'you know' that it will come into fruition.

Just as when you sow a seed,
'you know' that it will turn into a plant,
'you know' that it will give you flowers and
'you know' that it will provide you with its fruits
because you had sowed that fruit's seed.
See, it's so simple.

5. Create Your Own Fantasy World

Accepting and recognising the value of being in the space of 'I don't know', brings in a realisation that there exists an unknown space that we ourselves create and keep feeding. How?

Well, life as we know it, is limited – we live in a finite body, in a finite world that is limited in space and time. It is finite because it has a beginning, birth or creation, and an end or death. However, life is much more than we know it to be. There is a lot that we do not know.

'More than we know' is the space of 'I don't know', and we can believe that space to be magical. We can 'assume' it to be unbelievably fantastic, extraordinarily amazing and more of a fantasy world or a world that we envision for ourselves. And why not? We don't know what is actually in that unknown space, but we do have the power to influence it with our thoughts. So why don't we assume it to be amazingly magical?

Give this a thought: all fairy tales are a product of our imagination, and they take us to a fantasy or an imaginary world. So why don't we influence our so-called 'I don't know' world with magical fantasies? Not realistic, you say? So, what is realistic? What is real? The God that we interact with every day and the entire human race swears and lives by it, what is that? If we can live by that, we can surely live by creating a world of I don't know to a wow world – a wow future.

Here's something to think about: millions of people going around Mecca and millions of people in churches and temples are all following *'a belief'*. So why can't we create a wow fantasy world and believe it? It will come into fruition because it always does. Religion is proof of awareness, imagination, fantasy, and history turning into a belief system. Think about it.

There is limited or no proof of the occurrence of many event. We have not experienced it first-hand. However, humanity believes that these have occurred; people write books on them till date.

Isn't it true that we all continue to believe in something that we have not ourselves experienced? So why not choose our thoughts and create a life of our choice – our very own fantasy world? And if thoughts become things…wow!

Let's look at it in another way…
If thoughts are manifested as our reality,
if our thoughts and imagination create our reality,
then how does it matter if these events had occurred or not?

Where is the question of 'believing in its existence', in this finite world or not? These did exist in someone's mind, and it did exist in someone's imagination. Also, if thoughts become things then how does it matter where it existed – in someone's thoughts or reality?

Humanity has believed in learnings from such happenings/events till date and may continue to do so, as long as it finds merit and value in it, and until it chooses to stop believing it.

6. Feel the Freshness of Each Day

When flowers bloom, freshness is in it.
When the sun rises, freshness is everywhere.
Bring that freshness into you.

Let's change our momentum. Do everything differently. Let's come out of the same old habits and choose new ones. That's how you experience freshness.

A new beginning every day.

Here is another way to look at it. Life is a game of cards that you play with your mindset. Consequences of the game depend upon how you play your turn. Your turn always takes you somewhere; life too always takes you somewhere. You are never stagnant, not even for a millisecond. Days move into nights and vice versa. No two days and no two nights are alike; no two days are the same or make you have the same experience. Every day your life gives you fresh experiences, fresh days and fresh thoughts.

Choose your thoughts and start your new day, every day. It's not difficult. Think fresh, clear and clean.

That's why you start every day with a bath, cleaning yesterday off you. Try to shower your mind too in that bath and welcome the new fresh day. It's the best meditation ever.

Every day is a fresh new beginning. Isn't it marvellous?

7. Did You Know That You Are a Part of Universal Synchronicity?

The base of our body consists of cells that are in our tissues. These cells have memory. Our cells have molecules, and these molecules comprise of even smaller parts called atoms. All of these, each and every dot, move in a circular motion, just as the universe does, just as the galaxy does. It coincides with the earth, moon and stars. We all are in synchronisation with the earth, the universe and with the galaxy, becoming one with it all – this is Oneness. That is what is happening…

We are moving with 'all that is' together as one.

Let us imagine that we are aligned, synchronised and are moving with all that is. While visualising this, tap into all your desires and touch them. Feel good as if your desires have already been fulfilled.

Keep doing this and life will become 'so yummy'! Do not wonder or focus on how your desires will be fulfilled, just keep visualising and feeling good. Let's continue asking in this manner through visualisation and we 'will' receive. It is a process. Now, were we aware of this?

8. Where Do We Come From?
Does It Really Matter?

Water pouring out of a tap – what is the source of this water? A tap, the place where the water collects, the water tank or is it the place from where the water department gets water? Is it the sea or ocean, or is it the spring? Is that the source or is rain the source or mountain peaks, where the ice melts and becomes a river and flows into the sea or is it the clouds? What is the source of water? Evaporated sea or ocean water? Where is the source of a simple thing like water?

Well, some questions do not have easy answers. We can see and feel it but are not even aware of its source. That's because we have moved away, so far ahead in this existence that it doesn't matter. All we know is that we and all living things need water for survival, no matter what, irrespective of where it came from. This is the truth, and we must enjoy it.

So is life. Why are we all worried about how we came and where will we go? The essence of living is going away from our palm.

Live with joy and happiness,
enthusiasm and wonder,
and with gratitude and abundance.
It is the only way and the best way to survive and live.

Keep a smile and wonder: what will happen, now? What will unfold? You might be in for a surprise!

9. Why All This, You Say?
Why Not All This, We Say?

Life as we know it, is like a movie. It's just an experience where your higher self merges with this existence's experiences. It is! That's what life is. Your Oneness, you and the earth merging and then going on a road trip to a destination. Life is the experiences that one goes through whilst on this trip, that's all. Once you reach your destination, you merge with another existence and experience that new journey till one reaches the end of that destination, too.

Now in that new journey, you experience different pathways, different faces and their experiences, and the experiences of those people existing in those places. You merge with the experiences of those that you resonate with and become one. When you do not resonate with some of their experiences, you leave those or drop them there itself. You merge and then grow and continue to add on and move towards the end of the destination.

Why are these experiences required? What's the point of all this?

Fun!

Imagine – 'you' without your body. You can't touch, you can't feel, you can't smell, and you can't eat. That's like being in the spirit state where these are not needed and not required. Won't the possibility of feeling, touching, smelling, even healing be very exciting then? So, what would you choose then?

Why all this, you say?

Why not all this!

Think about it. These experiences are required to expand eventually, evolve and move further.

10. Why Can't Life Be Fun?

This life is so simple and easy if we believe and know it to be simple and easy. Life is so magical. Why can't we all see it as magic? If one looks at all the inventions and creations from the past up to now…wow. Life truly is magical. Why can't we concentrate on those aspects of life?

Life is a game if you choose to play. The earth is a board game, where the best player wins, the lucky player wins or the smart player wins. Is that so? Or is it that the one who is the most excited and enthusiastic about playing the game that wins? Then again, is it really about winning? What is the point of winning it with stress? The actual winner of the game is the one enjoying the game, isn't it? It's the same in life. The one winning or living the game of life is the one who is enjoying every minute of it.

Life is a pack of cards – Queens, Kings, and more. It is an easy game, and your heart feels free to play with these cards. Play it, be it, feed it, sleep it and feel it.

Remember, no matter what the circumstances were, Lord Krishna (mentioned in the *Gita*) made a huge war like the *Mahabharata*, a gameplay. He watched it as an observer. He was in it, but he actually watched it with detachment. Even if you are in the middle of circumstances that are not favourable towards you, detach and watch, knowing that it is just a game, and play with enthusiasm. It should be fun.

Perhaps we have chosen to come here in this reality to prove something to ourselves or just for the experience, and we have to live, no matter what the circumstances are. So why not make it fun! Let's have fun, smile and laugh as much as we can. Not easy, you say? How is being unhappy and sad serving you? It's better to live and act happy than to live believing that you are sad. How will sadness serve you? How will it help you live? Will it be a gift to you?

Life, my dear friend, is a gift. Gifts are only given during celebrations and not on sad occasions. If life is a gift, you must surely be in some celebration.

That's our fact – that's our reality. So let's enjoy the game of life as it is a gift and a celebration. Enjoy and acknowledge the gift, for you are the chosen one. The source had a choice, and it chose to create you. So let's celebrate and move on like a gameplay.

11. Why Not Enjoy the Game Called Life and Create Experiences?

Life is a game! Let's play the number game – emotions associated with numbers. You can associate an emotion with a particular number and play this game.

Take the number 9. There is a belief that the number 9 means life; 9 means abundance; 9 means support; 9 means perseverance; 9 means creativity and 9 means punctuality. Every time you spot the number 9, feel abundant, feel supported and feel creative.

You can play the game in another way, too.

Think of the number 6. Now think about yourself, your life and note which positive feeling or emotion stands out for you the most. Note it and associate the number 6 with that feeling. Henceforth, every time you spot the number 6, relive that feeling, instantly – the feeling that you had associated with number 6.

Alternatively, you can also do this…

When you are feeling 'extremely happy or excited', think of a number and associate that feeling to it. Say, for example, you have considered number 1. Now, whenever you come across number 1, you will recall the same experience or feeling that you had associated with this number – the feeling of extreme happiness. Soon, you will experience the same feeling each time you spot the number 1.

Play this game for a while.

12. Life Is a Gift. What Are You Doing About It?

Life is so simple and easy. All you have to do is know that all is well, and things will flow. You must know that the brilliance of life, of existence, brilliance in itself, is worthiness of self in existence, without ego, and with humility. It means that wonderful things will happen because I know it will.

Know and *knowing* are huge words. Know – you just know it. There are no strings attached to that word. There is no stress attached and no heavy energy attached to it. It's simple, yet brilliant – just as the stream knows that it will join the sea, so does life. So you see, nothing serious is going on here.

LIFE – the word itself, what does it mean? Can you feel the energy of that word? 'Life'… Wow.

Life means to live.

Life is plants, trees and leaves.

Life is animals.

Giving birth to life – to babies.

Do you know how massive the word 'life' is and how vast the *'intention of life'* is? Do we know the intention that went into creating that life? Do we? Say the word 'life' once more to feel it. Aah…Life!

Life is huge, and it is beautiful. It is brilliant and magnificent, too. Ah! If only we get what life is.

You will enjoy every step that you take;
you will enjoy every word coming out of your mouth;
you will enjoy every word you hear;
you will enjoy every food you taste;

you will love your caretaker, your breath;
you will love what you see in the mirror;
and you will love the earth, the wind, the sky, the flowers,
the birds and the cool breeze.

Aah! That is life and you have it – you have the gift of
life. That is *your* gift – yours – for you. Isn't that brilliant?
So, what are you doing about it?

13. Why Not Create and Then Marvel At It?

Life is a quest. A quest to create the unknown yourself, and then marvel at it or wonder about it. Unknown is a creation by you, and by every individual.

When you are thinking of the past, you are traveling into an unknown space using your imagination, as the past does not exist anymore. You do this when you are revisiting history. Do you want to think of the past? Great. However, remember, thinking of it is also feeding your unknown.

So why not create a beautiful unknown? Create it with passion and love.

This journey to the unknown is very simple. One can create it how one likes and that's the root, the base or the starting point. However, what do we actually do? We place fear at the base of the unknown root and then create a journey ahead. What kind of a journey would that be?

Why not create an unknown journey the way we would like it to be? What do we have to lose?

14. Why Not Be What You Desire?

When your capacity to flourish is limited, how will you truly flourish? Uh, really? Is this statement true?

Let's think about it. If you look at everything and every aspect of life from limited space and desire the abundance that exists in a gloriously abundant space, how can you reach there? How?

You have to be what you desire. You have to be it.

See yourself in it and ask beyond it, then can you be in that space of abundance and fulfilment of one's desires. You see, it's that simple: 'be in that space – be abundant'. Feel the feeling of being rich, and you shall be.

It's all about the vibrational place that one is in, you know. Let's make it clearer and simpler. You see, life as we know it has no boundaries, but man creates boundaries to protect his ego. Because of insecurities, weaknesses, fear of plagiarism; man is so scared of others taking or stealing what he has! What if you realise that it is all available in abundance and everything should be shared without regret?

The ones who do not share, 'Oh! Their energy is always full of fear. They are frightened and always wondering'. However, the ones who share, 'they are free, flowing, more peaceful, more loved and more loving'. One has to choose the kind of life one wants: one with boundaries or a free-flowing life.

The one who shares knows that he has it all and so he shares, for he knows that abundance, love and prosperity are continuous. It comes and goes and comes again. He knows that he will never be empty and will always have more than enough. Think, does the Source keep all the information to itself or is always trying to impart information? It's us human beings who do not trust nor believe in the Source. If the Source does not keep all the abundance for itself, how can you? You are as magical as the Source that has it all, always has and always will. If the Source continuously gives you, how will you fall short? It is not possible.

Wealth, health, prosperity is always there, always. Believe it – it's yours – Believe it.

This has to be an abundant experience and this life is definitely an abundant space to be in. We are gifted with a body, talents, perception and vision. We create, we judge, we build, we solve, we invent and we discover. Is all this possible without this body, without this experience and without this journey? We wonder. What do you think?

The body, soul, riches, gifts, all are gifts of abundance. People are always looking for abundance, forgetting that they already have abundance. It's something that you are born with – then what is asking, meditating and looking for abundance? You have already asked for it and it is a done thing – that's why you are here on this earth in this form, for this experience, because you had asked for abundance.

Earth, you in it, everything in nature: metal, wood and also your creations such as electronics, money, health, hospitals, homes, airplanes, trains and cars, all this is abundance. So where is the lack? Why can't we all see this? Why can't we all appreciate this and forget about the rest? Let's enjoy everything. All that is here on earth: enjoy the trees, the gentle breeze on your face, walking on the grass, breathing in the fresh air, the waterfalls, the streams, the beaches, the oceans, all that is abundance. Enjoy all that. It's easy.

Smile and walk under the sunshine, cherishing your life.

15. Do You Really Need a Purpose to Enjoy Life?

Why does everybody need a purpose in life? Does one need a purpose to enjoy life? Can't you just be life? Can't you just experience life?

You are here to experience life, that's it!

Look at the plants, flower and animals. Are they asking for a purpose to justify their existence? They are just enjoying and living to their full, aren't they?

Live life.
Do all that you desire.

16. Why Aren't We Appreciating More?

In this universe, there are many pathways. To move ahead, you need to choose a path. Our choice depends upon a lot of factors. Some of which are our knowing, fear, happiness and appreciation.

Appreciation – a big word! See, how magical life will be if you live by appreciating everything and everyone that you come across, and how you can change the world of those people and your world too.

Experiment for the next three days. Be attentive. Call it 'My Three Appreciation Days.' Appreciate everyone and every situation that you come across. See how magical your life will become. Every week, mark three days of your appreciation and just watch what happens. Ask your friend to do it too with you, so you all can correct yourselves just in case someone slips. After the first three days, write down what you felt. Three things that you felt. This is good, try it.

Appreciation is the best medicine to help people go to another level. With encouragement and appreciation, a person starts knowing his value. You cannot imagine where appreciation takes a person, to what levels and to what heights. It changes one's world. Try to appreciate others more, appreciate other's work and creation more.

Look for all that you can appreciate, even in a stance you don't like much. There has to be something that you can find to appreciate from that stance. One appreciation will take the creator of that stance, from what to where – it is sometimes unimaginable. So appreciation is necessary to soar.

Appreciate the Source for all that is
and then watch where you go.

First let's appreciate that 'which is', then move on to seeking that 'which isn't'. Life as you know it breeds life! So you see, there is nothing to it.

Life is to live, not judge. It is to experience.
Not to starve, but to eat in fulfilment.
Live in gratitude.
Before it is too late, live every bit, every second of it.
Do not overthink.
Just rejoice, be happy, enjoy things and enjoy the earth.
Enjoy this reality first,
then question and talk about spirituality.
First live this life.

Live for yourself as you are living for Oneness – for all that is.

Moreover, if you want to help people, first, help yourself. Live. Enjoy. You may not get another chance. Look at the flowers, watch television and look at the colourful clothes. Look at all that man has created, appreciate all that first and then go for the unknown. We human beings have created amazing things. Appreciate your kind first, be in gratitude of them first and then go off to the other realms. First, appreciate people, earth, humanity, their creation, then go elsewhere.

See everything as if you are seeing it for the first time: cars, trains, planes, buildings, home, plants, usage of water, electricity – Wow! Human beings are magical. They are indeed masterpieces! You, me and all of us.

17. If All Our Experiences and Beliefs Are the Same, What Is the Point of This Existence?

It all depends upon where you stand, how and which path of evolution you have taken. Paths taken by each soul is different. That's how you and I experience diversity.

Do you think that there is only one path and that there is only one dimension and one way? No way. There are enormous dimensions, enormous paths and enormous ways. How will then Oneness experience diversity? We need to think and understand who is doing who a favour? Who is experiencing for us to evolve: God, me or you?

Just think, if all our experiences and beliefs are the same, then what is the point of coming into this existence? If everything is the same, how will Oneness evolve and experience diversity? Experiencing diversity is very important for Oneness to evolve.

Hence, it is important in this existence for the rich to exist, coinciding with the poor and whatever is in the middle.

It is important for darkness and light both to exist.
It is important for people of different ethnicity to exist; good times, bad times and mediocre times to exist; happiness, sadness and boredom all are required to exist. The mountains, rivers and earthquake to exist and also for peace and harmony to exist.
All of it together: various dimensions, various existence, multiple emotions, and various perceptions; all that together help Oneness to evolve.

Oneness is such a huge and vast experience. How will you call it God or Universe or Oneness if it does not encompass all that exists? Only if it is experiencing everything and even beyond all that, in terms of emotions, in terms of relationships, in terms of physical, mental, spiritual and everything that you can think of, whether it is an ant, whether it is giant, an alien, whether it is evil, good, every drop…all of it and beyond our knowledge, consists of Oneness. You can only call it God if it has the experience of everything which is both possible and not possible. That's why diversity is so important.

The Source is like the head of the octopus and we are its hands – its tentacles. What we experience, the Source experiences. Source is constantly growing and evolving through our experiences. Think about it.

18. Rub the Lack

Rub the lack! The lack you feel in every stream of life, rub that lack. Once you rub the feeling of lack, it's all there.

In this world, one sees many dreams, loads of flowers bloom, countless stars twinkle and shine in the sky at night. What do you think, do they all just exist and do nothing? Do they just stand and look at you struggling? No. These are an important contribution to your life, too. Why not communicate with them, ask them, command them? Let's command the earth and command the universe. Do whatever pleases you, for they are all with you. They will move forward with you as you move ahead. They will make your situations comfortable.

Because this is life, it feels a little complicated. Lack of faith and lack of trust in themselves creates unpleasant experiences. However, the breath has the capacity to heal and give life and sustain life.

Ask the breath to heal it and it will. It is the sustainer.
Ask it to clean it and it will. It is a cleaner.
Ask the breath to restore because it restores. That's its work.
Breathe – try it. Your breath is within you, always.
Life is simple.
Find solutions in simple things, in simplicity.
One has to enjoy life selfishly, like a flower.
Enjoy and fly like a bird.
Enjoy and run like a deer.

Unpleasant experiences come from a feeling of lack. However, if one believes, *'heck it! I will have just fun, will speak fun, will be fun and experience fun'*, slowly and steadily he definitely will! Try it. Soon you will be attracting abundance and fun.

We human beings lack acknowledgement, trust, belief and knowing. Look at the tree; it is so deeply rooted in its knowing that only a huge typhoon can uproot it. However, it does not uproot all the trees. Only the ones that are weak, as they have engulfed themselves in fear, get uprooted.

Rub the fear – Rub the lack.
Be deep rooted and believe.

FLOW

19. Do You Want to Attain Complete Satisfaction?

You want and desire to evolve in order to create more, in order to experience more and in order to manifest more satisfaction?

Give me one person in this life who is satisfied? Even the person who says that he is satisfied is actually not satisfied.

This is because a quest for satisfaction, movement and looking further and going beyond is the only truth and reality.

Movement is the only truth.
There is no such thing as satisfaction.

20. Feeling Stuck? Think Again

Life as we know it, is fulfilling. We have it all here, yet we can't see it. We are stuck between good and bad, hell and heaven, liquid and solid. Not many of us are going with the flow. Long discussions with loved ones about right and wrong, good and bad are not needed. What's the point? Just flow. Experience life beyond 'the beyond' i.e. beyond your expectations, beyond your knowledge, beyond your perception and assumptions.

Everyone and everything wants to experience evolution. So, let us just flow and not stop to think. Don't stop to think why is it happening, how is it happening and what to do?

Whatever is happening, it should only get better. Keep your focus and continuity.

The more you discuss, the more you will fall back, and you will have to start again. Think *'I don't know where I am heading or how I am going (in terms of continuity). I just know that I am moving forward well'*. Keep going and moving further.

Why are you stuck? Improvement and evolution are inevitable and is natural law. This can be seen in non-living things and also in human beings.

We evolve and move forward – that's the law.

If you do not wish to move forward, then you have a choice to end it. But you will then feel *'Oh! Why didn't I try harder? I also want to move forward. I want to go back, so badly'*.

Moving forward is the only way – move on.

If only we all knew what we have. The Source does not have that at all, does it? That's why the Source has sent us here. It has sent us to abundance, wealth and health. So what are you doing about it?

Improvement, expansion and abundance will definitely take place – it is the law, like it or not. Just as at first, there was the TV, then came the internet. Just focus on improvement and expansion.

We are asking for abundance, wealth and money from whom or what? It all exists here, on earth. We all are living and experiencing these, here. These do not exist anywhere else. The experience of money – we have that.

So you are abundant, acknowledge it.

Isn't it funny that we human beings have it all here on earth, but we are blind and cannot see this fact, and we ask the Source or God for it and continue to ask. Ask yourself – ask the earth.

Live life with ease and understand life with ease and joy.

21. You Think You Can Stall Knowledge?

The cat always runs out of the bag.
You can't tame a cat and make it stay put.

So does knowledge. Knowledge can never stay put in a mind or in books, it will always flow. You cannot curb it and keep it only for you, it will find its own way. It will find its own takers.

Knowledge is incredible. It will find its way to spread. One cannot keep it stocked or stalled for long. Knowledge has to be imparted, that is its nature.

22. Life Is a Continuous Flow

Look at where the stream starts and what journey does it go through to be one with the ocean and to be a part of all those exquisite sea animals. Passion is a continuous flow that leads the stream into an ocean. Similarly, we are created as a cell to lead our lives in such a way that we end up being one with that ocean called Oneness.

So why be born then, when we were already a part of Oneness, before coming here on earth?

Before we are created, our vibrations and Oneness's vibrations are different to when we leave and join Oneness, after this reality's journey. It is continuous, never-ending and infinitely flowing. It has no beginning and no ending. Can you ever define a stream's beginning and end? Nope. Which crystal of water is ahead, and which is behind? Yes, but not the beginning nor end.

Try to think: when did it all start? Does it start when the frozen particles of snow turn into water and join the river or when the water evaporates from the ocean and forms clouds? Or is it when the water vapour pours down as rain on earth? There is no beginning – no end.

Flow Fearlessly!

The path that is resistance free, is the path that can take you to various possibilities where you can flow without any hitch. It is all in your hands. If you want to swim along with the flow, or flow along with the flow, or float along with the flow, the choice is yours. The river of life is flowing. Now how you want to experience it, that depends upon you. The river of life will flow and merge into expansion, into the sea and then into the ocean. But you see, we human beings are more comfortable swimming along the river, and we prefer to be by the shore when it comes to the sea and the ocean. Only diverse and great swimmers actually experience the sea or the ocean, the rest of us take a ship or a boat to experience the vast waters.

So you see, it's not that we all don't want to experience the sea or the ocean, we actually can't figure out which way the sea or the ocean flows. It is huge, looks stagnant and still, but it is definitely abundant with its own life and world – some discovered, some not yet discovered. But doesn't one experience peace in the ocean? Experience silence, peace and calmness till one experiences fear in that vastness – fear of sharks or fish etc. Fear messes up the peace in the ocean. So in order to enjoy the peace in the ocean, we need to discard fear, and then sit and experience the ocean; that's how life goes too.

Our life on earth is like the river; sea is the afterlife and the ocean is Oneness with all that is, the unknown and the unimaginable. Examples of this are all here in this existence, you just need notice it and understand.

Is life as we know it? Maybe. You have to see it and think it.

So keep moving... It is simple, yet it is a little complicated. Anything that is enormous, giant and enthusiastic (such as the Source) can create an enormous and giant enthusiastic reality. But people give up. They give up and then look for blame or where they went wrong, what they did wrong, or how they did it.

It's simple. Keep the enormous, gigantic enthusiasm on and on till you open the doors to the pathway of 'voila'. When you give up, you give up, that's it. But when you are persistent, you win.

Just imagine that this one life is a one-time gift to us and we all know that our time on earth is quite limited. Now knowing this, how would you desire to live your life? What can you do to live your life that way – your way? Stop! Do not let any doubt or negative thoughts creep in. You have lived most of your life in fear and doubt, why not try a different approach? What have you got to lose? Try something different. Focus and think! How can you live the rest of your life in joy, happiness, passion and enthusiasm? Be delusional, if you have to for a while. You have nothing to lose.

So just flow…

People are making simple things complicated. Existence is the basic epitome of reality. Existence is the only key to tasting existence. To exist is itself a natural and a supernatural deed. Enjoy the gift of existing in this reality. Appreciating everything, everyone and every situation, honouring self and encouraging self and others, making this reality a bliss and is all that we, as mankind, should concentrate on. There should not be any thought or doubt about it.

A stream, a flow of stream, flows in one easy direction. It does not say, 'oh! I am turning back, or going back to my past, where my flow was affected by a stone, let me go there and push it down and come back as then I will flow better'. A stream just flows; it does not say, 'let me go and see how I was created'. It's just 'laa-dee-daa, dee-daa' … flows and keeps on flowing. That's it. Its crystals in that flow of water do have an existence and they keep on flowing, changing shapes, as they express their feelings by changing its shape, but that does not affect the flow of one stream, along with the crystal drama; it just flows. So you know that all will pass; flow, regardless of how you feel.

Hmm. So it's true when we say 'this shall also pass!' It will all pass regardless of all the challenges that we face in our lives. Life will go on, won't it?

23. Emotions

Emotion is at the core, even at the very beginning when all this had started. Emotion is the highest creator. Imagine a human without emotions. Could he thrive, could he choose, would he evolve? No.

Emotions create laws of nature, life and death, dramas, relationships, stress and push you from your core to evolve or else, what's the point? What's the point of living? What is the point to even choose to come to this reality?

Staying up there ________________________ didn't do much for you, so you chose to come to /\/\/\/\/\/\/\/\/\/\/\.

24. Keep on Moving

Life treats people how they treat life. It's simple. Go to the basics. You want to expand and go to the space of beyond, isn't it? Then why do you keep going back?

You move forward and the rest will follow.

You are moving ahead, others will learn. Life is moving in all directions and dimensions. It is continuously moving, isn't it? So move with it. Enjoy it; nourish it; and have fun with it, for you don't have much time. You have one life to live.

Expand it from a line.

Move and be brilliant with it, for yourself. Take yourself where no one has gone and enjoy the magnificent magic.

Don't wait for anyone. You move.

How? By being you. By reading, learning, thinking, walking and enhancing life. Enhance it. Be spirited and adoringly enhance your skills and blessings. Make people melt, to want to choose to be you.

If you are here at one place and you wish to be there in another place...Well! Congratulations then, you will have what you ask for. It is inevitable. It is but obvious and it is possible. One gets whatever one dreams of or desires. The important thing is that one needs to desire it, that's all.

25. Isn't Your Life as Per Your Perception?

Brilliance of imagination,
creation through imagination and desires,
wow, brilliant manifestations!
Creation…
Imagination of creation,
manifestation of the imagination of creation
leads to evolution and abundance.
Creation – Brilliant creation!
Imagination of creation is evolving, too.
Wow. Abundant manifestation. It's a cycle.

Isn't everything a cycle? Circular movement? You want to get out of this circular movement? Not yet. Right now, your reality is circular. So are you, you are made of circular components. So is the earth and the universe, everything in it is made of circular movement. Chain, food chain, weather cycle, earth going around the axis, universe movement, you can't go beyond circular movement. That's your reality.

Life as we know it is vulnerable yet strong, easy yet hard, exaggerated yet teeny-weeny; it's all your perception, where you stand and where you are.

Angels, masters, the Source, the idea of it all, is wonderful, amazingly exciting, but when you think of the Source and pray, and you request the Source, the Source contributes to you. Once the Source decides to contribute to you, then all in the Source has to contribute to you as well, as it is the decision and mercy of the Source to contribute to you.

Go beyond the beyond. But without belief, how will your beyond stand a chance? If you do not believe that there is something for you beyond the beyond, then how can you and why will you desire to go to the beyond?

We are always looking for success and happiness. Two main important paths of our journey in this existence are happiness and success. Water flows without looking for happiness or success. That's because success is inevitable. The stream will join the river and the river will join the sea and it's inevitable, it is true. If you view YOU from the bigger picture, you are just a crystal in the stream of water.

We have blindfolded our eyes; we don't give our reality any significance. We are breathing, walking and talking. Let's compare ourselves to an animal or a flower and then try and see and sense our achievements.

If we realise that at the end, we are just a crystal in a stream that will join the river no matter what – will join the sea no matter what; will join the ocean no matter what – so where is the reason to be stressful? It is a waste of time, isn't it?

26. How Can We Win Over Pain?

One can understand life with ease and joy. Live life with ease.

What about victory over pain, you ask?

Have patience and tolerance. You are not the only one going through pain. This is a process – if you trust, you create. When you trust, you create possibilities and new beginnings. Pain will pass. It will become less with time and learning, and healing will take place. It is inevitable!

Yes, constant pain on daily basis is doing no good! One gets used to constant pain. In the beginning, it has more fear attached to it but as time passes by, there is acceptance. It is made a part of life. Life goes on and does not stop. Pain is never forever! It just pricks and goes away. Nothing is permanent. Everything and everyone moves.

Movement depends upon the thoughts that we choose.

Believing and thinking takes us to possibilities. The earth is going through whatever it is going through, all because of fear. People swear by religion and God, but don't actually believe and trust it, that's a fact. It is in our reality.

Belief and trust will sail the boat. Doubt will wriggle the boat and fear will make it sink. Trust and belief will create miracles and magic.

27. Movement Is the Only Truth

Right or wrong? You are right, there is confusion regarding which path to take. But you should know that you are always right, if you think you are right.

What is wrong, what is right? Let's just play the game of life and create our own right and wrong – or you can say, let's just choose our experience. Every choice that we make, or every experience that we choose, will lead to a certain consequence. We have to decide that if we want to continue moving in the same path, is that consequence right for us and acceptable to us? If yes, then move on accordingly. If the consequence does not do anything for us, then we can always choose something else. Sometimes, if you tag your experiences as right or wrong, the journey goes off trail. For a smooth sailing, all you have to do is move, move anywhere – just move.

Movement is always ahead.
Just move, don't judge, it's not needed.

Right and wrong takes you into another drama. You derail from your path then and you create a house or a community at the side of your path and keep on expanding it by trying to sort things out. You get stuck in the drama of right and wrong and keep getting entangled into its web and are unable to move forward.

Instead, just say, *I don't know if it is right or wrong. Maybe it is, maybe it is not the best option'*, and move on, nevertheless. Don't stop – move, just move, go, go, go. Make the journey of uncertainty exciting!

Then instead of living in fear, make a lovely movie, where you have the gift of imagination. Create it and make it real. Live your fantasy or imagined world; better than living in fear and frustration which will derail you. Move without doubt, smile and move, enjoy every move and dance every few minutes. Switch on the music and 'give life to your life'. The body is made to move, and it just moves. It does not say, '*This way is wrong, or oh! I should move that way*'; the body just moves. It has an intention to move, that's it. Rest of the body parts do what that they are intended to do. Life is simple.

GPS

Always say 'what else is possible' and be in that space. There is a difference between words and action but believing will bring them together. You see, there is a difference between 'when you believe where you stand and how you feel' and 'when you don't believe where you stand and then how you feel'.

You have to walk to a path of belief. When you are not in the path, what would you do? Look at the GPS, won't you? When you drive and lose your path, what does one do? Switch on the GPS.

So all you have to do is switch on the GPS and move on to the 'path of belief'.

Now, how do you switch on your GPS?

By being happy, being content, with satisfaction, and a smile, listen to nice talks, watch funny stuff or read a book. Switch on the GPS of your happy path. When sad or in doubt, say 'let's switch on my GPS' and do it imaginatively.

Create a change by being the change.

Create the change by being the change and then change, by being here and now. Our job is to bring this reality to a change and move. That's it. We have to live and walk our talk. Even if one person changes because of you? Wow, then how many will you influence to change.

Fear is predominant in our society. Move forward even with fear and fear will automatically go away. Trust your path and keep your GPS on, always.

MAN THE MARVEL

28. Switch the Off–Button in Your Head

What is life? Is it an accomplishment? Let's look at all that we have accomplished here in this existence. Is everything that we have added on to ourselves so bad? Is it? Is it negative, really? We can walk, talk, touch and feel.

Feel – even if one can't walk or talk, the human being has 'feelings'. That feeling, 'oh! It is so precious'.

Pay attention to your feelings.

Sometimes, sense it and see if that particular feeling will help you to move further to evolve and to grow. And if it does not? (There is no such thing). Drop it. Drop that feeling. And how do we drop that 'not-so-yummy' feeling? By switching the off button in our heads – that's it. Distract ourselves and move on.

Look for a feeling that will help us to evolve, to move ahead and to pass the difficult phase or time.

29. Concept of Time

Do you think that man has created time and the concept of time? Man did not create day and night; the Creator created it. Man just became aware, became conscious of this cycle, and he began understanding it and started using it for his ease.

Time is just a magical creation for us human beings to acknowledge our progress.

Time is such a delight, such a discovery, and such an innovation! It is because of time that we as human beings can acknowledge and value self, value existence and value success and for that matter, even acknowledge what success is.

Time is an inspiration. If human beings could actually discover time, one of the biggest secrets of creation, imagine what else exists that human beings have yet to discover or find.

Source Creates, You Unfold

Undoubtedly, there is so much more hidden, waiting to be revealed. It is said that nature itself houses a lot of universal secrets that we can observe by just being fully present and conscious. Life is indeed a treasure hunt, let's play this game and unfold its well-kept secrets.

30. Isn't Man a Marvel?

Life as we know it, is fascinating. Actually, we are not aware of how fascinating life is. Just wonder how the nomads had lived? How people had lived without electricity? How people had lived without cars? It's fascinating how humans have used their awareness, capacities and capabilities, acknowledged that they had these capabilities and capacities to create wonder and have brought life to what it is. Human beings have done this, haven't they?

Imagine a person from the past, from the time the wheel was invented. If he was to come here to our present world, he would be completely lost and in awe of everything.

Nature has progressed too but look at what man has created for himself and has used the help of nature to create, evolve and develop further? Man has done all that. Compare the progress of man and the creation of man to the progress and creation of nature. Do you get me?

Man is far more than he gives himself credit for. He finds the solution, he finds the process, he cultivates all to magnificent outcomes, isn't it? So are we living our lives as we know it? Is it justifiable to always put man down? Is it justifiable to give the credit to the power of who or what we can't see? Should we not thank our kind (mankind), to have spent time to think about us all (human beings), to have given us a better and comfortable life, to have made life easy for us? We have that power. We are creators who have all that abundant power. Proof is all over as soon as you open your eyes. So don't worry, for all the solutions lie here. Of course, we do require the entire universe and beyond to contribute to us, but the real solution lies in our hands, in your hands.

31. Aren't You a Masterpiece?

The Creator knows the capacity of its creation; the artist is aware of his skills. He knows and has confidence in his creations and that is why he is called an artist. So the creator is aware of his artwork, but is the art piece aware of its capabilities or worth? Nah! Same is the case with human beings. The Creator knows his creation (a human) and is aware of his capacities, capabilities and worth, whereas mankind does not.

Man is aware of his Creator and considers him unapproachable, unreachable, and he doubts everything. Just like the art piece, this gap between the Creator and the creation has to be removed, rubbed, eradicated and made non-existent.

How does one do that? By believing and trusting.

Let's figure this out step by step and one by one. Beautiful and lovely, we are part of the Source, aren't we? So what is the problem? Then why don't we all get it that we are a part of the Source. There is nothing more to tell if you are part of the Source. Who are you, what are you, where are you, why are you, for whom are you, for which are you and then how are you, etc. does not matter. If you are a part of the Source, then no further explanation is required.

Creation or mastermind creates only a masterpiece, isn't it? Does the masterpiece know that it's a masterpiece? No. We make it a masterpiece because we are awed by it. A masterpiece can be a creation of a mastermind only, isn't it? What will it take for each one of us to know that we are masterpieces? We are created by the mastermind, so we are masterpieces.

Walk like a masterpiece;
Talk like a masterpiece;
Live like a masterpiece.

The Creator or Source who created the mountains, rivers, oceans, also thought that you were required, so He created you. The Source is the artist and we are Its creation – Its masterpiece.

So let's see if we got it right. We are acknowledging and giving credit to the Creator who is the mastermind that has created us – His masterpieces (human beings) and we in turn are creating our very own creations – our masterpieces. So actually these messages are giving value to both the Creator and the creations, aren't they?

Let's look at it another way: when we all celebrate the national day of our country, we can see the national flag flying high all over the country. Now, what is a national flag? The representation of the country – a sign of the country. The national flag is the representation of what the country stands for. It represents everything that the country has gone through. It has a story attached to it and it flies high up in the sky, dances in the wind – even to the national anthem. People don't move to it and yet it rejoices up there, knowing its worth and flies – moves happily with freedom and in its full glory, doesn't it? It is a representation of the entire country collectively, together – irrespective of everything… caste, creed and religion. It is respected, saluted at, and the flag enjoys all this with pride.

Now what are you? Who do you represent? Who created you? You are a representation of the Creator and you feel ashamed in praising yourself, in praising your capacities, capabilities and qualities and you call that humble. Really?

You are a true representative of the Creator, God, Allah, Buddha, the Source. You are a masterpiece, you should respect yourself more than the flag, shouldn't you? You are a collective consciousness – you should keep yourself as high as the flag, rejoice and enjoy your existence. You represent all that the Creator stands for.

Let's look at the life of Buddha. He represented humbleness, simple life and simplicity. He took pride in himself and his existence. He didn't judge. He did what he did and reached to people in the best way that he thought he could. Is it possible to doubt self and teach people all that he had taught? No. So let's snap out of doubt, fear, jealousy, cheapness and complain. Let's live a rich life knowledge-wise, love-wise and happiness-wise.

32. You Are Spectacular

Spectacular – What a word! It has so much in it. Why can't everybody ask for 'spectacular'? Each and every one of us is spectacular? Why can't we all see, how spectacular we all are? From where we (the authors) see it – wow, you are spectacular!

You can write, eat, walk, talk, smell, see, hear and have awareness. Wow! This is as spectacular as it can get. You can feel, sing, laugh, cry, feel, pain, feel joy, jump, sit and stand. Wow! You can dress up, feel shabby, be happy, get depressed, cry tears, giggle and dance. Wow, you can do so much. Spectacular, isn't it?

You can sleep and then wake up, be fresh, comb your hair, you have a pet – your body to take care of, and it goes with you everywhere. It's spectacular. Polish nails, take a beauty bath and drink water. Wow, spectacular.

And you think Burj Khalifa's fireworks (in Dubai) are spectacular? That's just light and fire to thrill you. But who created it? You (mankind) did. The creator of that is spectacular. We should kiss the hands of those who created all that for all of us to enjoy. We are spectacular!

Let's see each and every human being today that we come across as spectacular. See how amazing life will be then. Let us consider everything and everyone in our house spectacular and see how they light up. Even consider everything that we throw out of our body as spectacular, as it came out of your body. This pen, ink, book – wow, spectacular.

So when you ask the Source for something spectacular, you are it!!! You don't even know it. If only we all knew; if only we all realised.

Realise it! Give it a thought, O Spectacular!

33. You Are Awe

So what now? You wonder and enquire with so much zeal and enthusiasm. Why don't you live your life in that energy, that passion? What good will laziness and lethargy do? Just live a little. Your days on earth are numbered, so live them with enthusiasm, joy and passion. Enjoy the essence of life, of living, of receiving, of belonging…just live a little this way.

You repeatedly ask the Source for something awe-inspiring. Well, come out of the same old rut and ask for newness – new experiences. You wish to experience beyond the beyond, but you are always asking the same questions. How will it be possible then?

Well, you are awe! When will you realise that you are awe? Let's be a little clearer now. You are seeking, looking and thinking about awe – hence, you are awe. That's why you are thinking and looking for awe. Let me explain further – it's clear that you always look for who you are; there is always a connection between who you are and what you are asking for. You cannot ask for something that you don't know. Can you even imagine a colour that you have never seen? You can only ask for something that you know the feeling of having or what you are familiar with through your knowing or experience.

You 'are' that, so you are asking for it – you just are not aware of the fact that you are that. Because if you didn't know how it feels to be that and have that, you would not ask for it in the first place, would you? So when you are asking for something, first acknowledge the fact that you are that what you are asking for – Awe! Where is the need for asking? You seek awe; you are awe.

Step one is the feeling of having it.

Step two is asking for it.

Step three is realising, 'Oh! I am asking for it, so I know what it feels like, to have it. Ah! Never mind, I know (have) it already. So, what's next?'

See, it is so simple. Do not complicate things. Life is easy – you are already what you are asking for.

Live, people. Live.

34. Focus on Your Capacities and Capabilities

This existence does not actually ask a lot, and this is true and factual. But people and their assumptions do. Life is and can be simple! People actually complicate things by assuming and putting a stamp on their assumptions, believing and then living by it, and then making 'that' their reality.

It's time to assume 'awesomeness', putting a stamp on it and living by it. What's the harm? Go into the 'I don't know' space again, influence it by positive thoughts, assume awesome possibilities and let's create awesomeness, what say?

You know that we all have capacities. We all have amazing capabilities that are similar and yet different. So what are we doing with all our capacities? We first have to know what our capacities are and for that we have to try new things all the time; walk a fresh new path all the time; and move away from our safe zone to a fresh new zone. How else will one know about the various capacities and qualities that one has? Living life in just one way, in one particular way, is that existing? No! In order to flourish, one has to experience different ways of existing. And for that, one has to come out of his or her comfort zone. One owes it to 'self'. Can't we all do at least this much for ourselves?

Write a list of a few things that you cannot imagine yourself doing. Take one task at a time and experience it. You might enjoy and love some, and you might hate and despise some. It's okay. It's fine. You are just getting to know yourself, that's all. In this manner, you will get to know your qualities, capacities and create possibilities for yourself.

Whenever you think and feel that you are stuck in life, which is a plain simple lie, just make a list of simple, new to-do list of new experiences that you have never imagined experiencing. Create that list and as a result, you will gather a new list showing your capacities.

TRUTH

35. Be True to Yourself

Be true to yourself, that's it, the rest is just drama. Nothing else is important and nothing else works.

Know who you are first and be true to yourself.

Life is a stream…
Flow, flow, flow and join,
Flow and join bigger and better seas,
Flow and join… continuously flowing,
don't look left or right, just flow…
Flow, its dynamics (underlying forces) are to flow, that's it.

You are powerful!
Know your strength within and flow in peace,
confidently and believingly.

Where are you caught up? It's nothing!
Why so much restlessness? It's nothing!
You are more powerful than you think.
So be who you are… dynamic, full of zest and enthusiasm! And play, enjoy, move forward and go beyond.

36. Illusion

It is so simple and easy. In inculcation (instil an attitude, a habit or idea by persistent instructions) of this existence, this reality, life as we see it, as we perceive it, as we know it, is mind-blowing and mind-boggling. When one has lost the passion for existence, he or she has forgotten the gift that he or she is gifted with.

Life is to be carefree.
Life is to give no meaning and no reasoning to anything.
Life is living in the 'I don't know' space.

Assumptions and perceptions are deceptive and are an illusion. That's why it is said that this reality is an illusion. Because it is. Because nothing is structured and within the foundation and with barriers; nothing as a matter of fact is that way. It's only our illusion. We need to come out of our illusion and see. Come out of all that point of view and voilà, we will fly to greater and wow possibilities. Illusion is us, our creation. Experience is what we have come here for. But we have made our illusions, facts and then we sit on it. Think about it.

Take the example of the time when we mistake a rope for a snake or when we see a mirage when there is no water. We do experience seeing the snake and water in both the instances whereas in reality these are absent. Similarly, our perceptions and assumptions shape our personal reality.

37. What Is the Truth?

So, what is 'truth'?

So much drama over truth, so much commotion over truth! Truth is also a judgment, isn't it? Just look at yourself and that is the only truth. You are truth. Use it. Speak your truth always.

Truth is momentary. For that moment, that is your truth, that's it. You choose your truth. Your truth has everything to do with you. What's the point of searching for a truth elsewhere, as it will never be your truth; it will be the other person's truth. Truth evolves as you evolve.

Today, this is your truth; few years down the line as a result of new experiences and new learnings, you may hold a completely different view, and then that would be your truth – and that's okay.

Also, what is true for me may not be true for someone else, as our truth is based on our experiences, beliefs, perceptions and our understanding. Take the example of that famous image in which half of the audience sees it as the face of a young girl, and the other half sees it as an old lady. Whose truth is real here? Both. We know that both sets of people saw what they claimed to see and yet their truths differ. Similarly, in life, often there is unnecessary chatter and dispute over who is right and who isn't.

Life is too magnificently huge and houses everyone's truth. Just because we are familiar with our truth, can we really disregard someone else's truth, because we can't see it?

Haven't we all experienced situations where we know we are right, and we spoke our truth, however, the other person had a completely different truth based on his or her experience, understanding and perception? And both were

hell-bent upon trying to prove their own perspective? Well …
Ahem.

38. I Know Me, It's Enough

Proving yourself right and the other wrong? What is the deal, anyway? You are awesome, he is awesome, and she is awesome, any which way, anyway. Why is there the desire to be right, to be superior, to be better? Why? What is the need for that?

Just be you…
You know you.
As long as you know you, it is enough.

You know you, that's it. Once you know you, the want to justify, fight, argue will not be needed. Be like the people who know themselves.

Once you know the gift that you are, you do not require to give any explanation. No need for any conversation, no need for any drama, just know self properly and have clarity in yourself. Have clarity in self, that's it – nothing else is needed.

39. A New Year Resolution

During a new year, a year ends, and a new year begins. New dreams, new desires, new aspirations come alive, come forth and come into existence. Bravo!

Instead of creating New Year's resolutions,
why don't we talk about what we have achieved
by the end of the previous year?

Then and only after that, let's welcome the new year and create new resolutions. Usually people look at what they didn't or couldn't create for themselves; they ask for a new year's space that they would like to be in and create their new year's resolutions.

How about thanking all that we have created in the previous year? And then ask for more for the following year? Wouldn't that be yummy?

40. The New Truth

Let us imagine a crystal of water flowing along the stream. Now, how does that crystal evolve and move further? Once it comes across a stone, does that stop its flow? Does it ever stop its flow? No, it still flows into the sea. That is inevitable. At the most, it will evaporate and have another reality. It may turn into a cloud and fall somewhere as rain, but its journey will go on without a point of view, wouldn't it? Point of views such as it has gone through suffering in its path, by being hit constantly against innumerable rocks, experiencing freezing temperatures, etc. It just merrily flows along the stream, doesn't it?

Similarly, just as the crystal flows in water, whilst on our journey, enthusiasm and excitement will lead us too, evolving us further. It will, that's the law of life – evolution.

The new truth is: Be happy and evolve.

Contrast is not working anymore. It is giving heartache and pain, that's why happiness is the new mantra. Think happiness – happy thoughts. Do small, insignificant actions that give you joy, that make you smile and that make you giggle. Make it a habit, and soon it will become your nature. First, do it deliberately, then it will become YOU.

We beings have been asking to be happy since eternity and it is flowing down into our vortex now. Let's keep our buckets ready and fill them with happiness. It's so simple: time for a change – time to be happy.

It's going to be all about happiness.
Happy. Joy. Fun. It's inevitable.

CREATION. ENDLESS POSSIBILITIES.

41. Creation Is Infinite

The finiteness of life is a limitation. The infiniteness is
actually what takes you further.

Think about this, is there any such thing as finite?
Everything, every molecule, every creation is infinite.

Let's examine…

Tree: wood to table or chair or door or house;

Leaf: leaf to nest or nest back into earth;

Fruit: food to creating and sustaining a body… Come on,
what is finite?

Earth? Don't even go there. There are so many
possibilities to earth. Creation of human bodies, trees,
buildings, gold, diamond, water… come on! Is there
something that is finite? There is only 'infinite creating
possibilities'.

Imagine what else can be created. There is so much yet to
invent, so much yet to discover.

42. Create Your Destiny Beyond the Beyond

A person who goes out to create his destiny will always find a way to create it. How he creates his destiny depends upon his frame of mind, his belief system, his trust and faith in himself. When it's clear for him what he wants to create as his future, it will clearly be visible to him eventually as destiny.

Loads and loads of possibilities exist, one just has to go beyond the end point, the so-called marginal end point. Once you are aware that you have reached the end point of something, voilà, that's when you go beyond from there, beyond the end point. How you ask?

By knowing and believing that something else has to be there beyond this point.

This point is fictitious and is an assumption as something beyond always exists.

43. Change Is the Effervescence of Life

It's true that life can be as amazing or more than brilliantly amazing, if you want it to be.

Life is creation and creating. That's it.
It means 'creating' and 'going on creating'…
No judging, no discussing, but creating.

Creators are leaders and discoverers are followers. Let's go to the energy of a creator, then go to the energy of a discoverer as both are needed and both are required. If you do not discover what is created, then there is no point of the creation, right? A follower is also a requirement of existence. Both creators and discoverers are connected in life.

This does not mean that a creator will always remain a creator and a discoverer will never switch his role with the creator; it can be vice versa, anytime. The discoverer can also take his discovery to another level of creation and become a creator, too. And then the creator has no choice but to be in awe of the now *new* creator.

This reality doesn't solidify the roles and expect individuals to play that role throughout. It's never like that.

For instance, a father is also a child, also an uncle, also a friend, also a president and also a husband. Everything and everyone in this reality plays different roles at different times of the day, depending upon their situations. *Let it be, don't judge.* See what role suits him best, at that moment. He is playing the part only for that time.

Nothing is the same forever, is it?

44. Reality Is What We Create

It is so natural to misunderstand our aim and goal for existence. It's not as superficial as we imagine. But then the question is, what is real? Exactly what is real? What answer do you have for this question? What is your reality?

Reality is what you create and how you create – from your mind, your imagination, your ideas, your perception, your creativity, your action and implementation – that leads to reality.

How you wish to live your life depends upon you. It also depends upon how much you can push your imagination further and how much you can move to the unknown space and create from there. Let's make that unknown space, known space.

Let's not judge anyone else as losers nor anyone as useless. If Albert Einstein could do it, then anyone can do it. We all are born with the same capacities and capabilities; the only difference is choice and perseverance. That's all.

45. Every Second Is Life

Well, what do you think? In life, we have loads of opportunities that take us in various directions. These directions have loads of things happening every second and every minute.

A second is a compilation of loads of happenings and thus every second is actually huge. Each second is created by experiences, expectations, judgement, results, emotions, values and so on. So every second that you live your life is as huge as life itself.

Be aware of every second for a bit. Monitor what every second says. Every second compiled together makes a minute, every minute complied together makes an hour, and every hour so on and so forth makes life, but that millisecond is also life. There is so much to it, as so much has happened in that second. The earth has moved, and planets have changed their positions in space. See, it is huge. People have given birth and have left the existence, too, in a second.

What is life for a flower? What is life for a seed? What is life for a petal? Every second counts for them, doesn't it? Life is inclusive of every second and every second is magical as so much happens in every second. What is life for an ant, for a mosquito or for a moth? That is also life. What is a cloud's life like? It destroys itself and adapts another form, rain.

Well, what to say? Is life an experience or is it an aftermath of experiences and expectations? Water forming as rain has another form but that form also is life, isn't it? Life changes every second; it can change its position, its form and its existence every second. Oh! This life is full of possibilities and happenings. The Big Bang Theory, just a second must have taken for that huge ball to realise: 'I cannot hold on to this anymore, I need to burst out and create life'. Just like a cloud that cannot take another drop anymore and that one extra droplet makes it burst out into rain. All takes place in a split of a second. Life is magnificent, is huge, and it is a split of a second, too. Isn't it?

46. Endless Possibilities

There are specific realms that one has to experience, you see. These realms are so exuberant and philosophically challenged that the philosophical aspect of life needs to shower in these realms. It has to be a balance of philosophy, existence, experience, circumstances, scientific research, and the end result that leads to the creation of NEW. It's a cycle. So you see, every realm of life has this cycle and more, loads and loads more.

One cannot limit life. Just try and imagine the life of an ant and its experiences, all the way to the animal kingdom and then to the human experiences. There are so many aspects, so many dimensions, roads, journeys and experiences to all, aren't there? How can we limit life to just us and our personal experiences? That's not life, that is just my own life; so how can I make my very own personal life, LIFE – a larger aspect. Think about it.

You see, life is and has to be unanimous and unimaginable, vast and huge but human beings narrow it down to just one individual's life. We have to understand that each and every individual lives his or her life in a different way, with different experiences, different mind-sets, emotions, religions, philosophies, etc.

We say that life is what we are living i.e. one individual. Why don't we see that whatever the population of earth is, that many possibilities exist in life; that many experiences exist; that many emotions exist; there are that many ways to live life and more! Why don't we go to that space of thinking and live our lives with so many possibilities? Different ways of living life – there are so many possibilities.

What is life for us? Our lives! We conclude life to be what we are experiencing, what we are going through and that is life for us. But no, life is the number of people existing in this universe, on this earth – each of who has a separate life. Life is the number of human beings that exist on this earth. So life is so many possibilities and possibilities are all those people existing on this earth, too. For a poor man, life is poor but for the rich man, life is success and happiness. What is life for a rich man such as George Clooney and what is life for a beggar and so many people between them? So life is all that and more. What is life for the children and the queens and the sheikhs? All that is life, too – so, so many possibilities.

Life also encompasses animals, birds, insects, microorganisms, etc. Imagine how many possibilities are then there for LIFE.

JUDGEMENT

47. Eliminate Excuses
and Complaints

Life as we feel it, or presume that we know it, is simple. Compassion and dedication lead to results. One has to live life as per these lines:

$$\text{Interest} \rightarrow \text{Dedication} \rightarrow \text{Passion}$$
$$\rightarrow \text{Desire} \rightarrow \text{Achievements}$$

So, first a person develops a slight interest in something. Once he is interested in it, he dedicates his time to it. Once dedicated, he realises that he is enjoying what he is doing, and it becomes his passion. He becomes passionate towards it. Soon, it turns into desire and he desires to take it further and evolve further and see if he gets any fruits as a result of his effort and action or if he gets any recognition. Then when he receives appreciation and recognition, that becomes his achievement.

There is no place for excuses or complaints. Once excuses and complaints become a part of your path, you know that then the barriers start rising. To eliminate the barriers, eliminate the excuses and complaints.

Look for questions, pathways to tackle a situation and go to what else can be done here and now?

48. The Recipe of Life

So you see, in life there are a few paths that one has to cross before his desire erupts or comes about. In order to fulfil those desires, he has to create some combination of feelings, emotions, wants, happiness, fun, adventure, material, goods, etc. to satisfy the desire. Say for example, to create a good meal, a recipe is required. One has to mix and match ingredients, then taste it to create a final dish, isn't it? So is life. To create a life, lots of aspects have to be considered and lots of things, emotions and circumstances have to be mixed and matched to create a tasteful life. But again, it all depends upon the taste of the person who is tasting the dish or life, you see. His background, his likes and his dislikes, and his experiences. One person might love the dish but if you ask some other person to taste the same dish, he might go 'yuck, not nice', or he may add something else to make it tastier for him.

So life, my dear friend, is not one person's liking. Desires of life can be similar to others. Doesn't mean that it is wrong. One individual wants to taste life in one way while the other wants to taste it in another way. So where does judgement stand here? There are individuals judging people creating their lives as per their liking, but they forget that the taste and experiences of the judges are also different. It is similar to a cooking show – that is actually how we all are living, the way we feel is right for us.

Is it actually valid then to judge life for the creation of all? Is it? Think about it.

Circumstances, situations, happenings, emotions, feeling, desires… everything constitutes and creates the life of a person. So one person's experience will create certain set of taste buds, while the other person's experiences in life will create another set of taste buds and the one who is judging, his experiences would have another set of taste buds, too. And we are comparing or judging one individual's taste buds and his creation to our taste buds which are completely different. So how can one judge the other?

Every individual has his own taste, give him that.

Every individual creates his own recipe of life, give him that.

You will learn your own recipe by observing, trial and error.

Create your own life.

It is an experiment that you are living; be an observer and then create. You kill life by judging.

What do you want the recipe of your life to be? Or do you want to change it on a daily basis? Think about this.

No Labels. No Judgement

Make your life simple and easy.

Let us share a story with you. It will help you get an idea of the message that we are trying to convey. We will begin by describing the place to you.

Many years ago, this place had mountains, waterfall, greenery, fresh air, flowers, rocks, ditches, mud, puddles, sky, cloud, rain, slippery pathways, butterflies, crows, eagles, birds, reindeers, lions, ponds, fish, seagulls, whales, urchin… and they all lived together.

The flowers didn't say, '*Oh, my God! There is this horrible insect on me*', or '*Oh, my God! Mud and puddle all over and it is stinking*'. The deer didn't say, '*Wow, rain – oh no! My God, dirty smell, yuck. Uff*'. This and that, Ying and Yang, all lived happily! None of them actually judged each other or gave each other a label. All just lived – just lived.

This reality, your reality, our reality, has so much space that Ying and Yang can live together without any judgment and without being labelled. So let's live on. Be happy! Be like the flowers and the birds. And if there are some ditches and mud puddles, so be it. That was because of the rain and these will eventually dry up. You just have to know it, just like the the animals on land, the birds in the sky and the fish in the oceans do. Nothing serious is going on here.

Live and let live and let go!

Forget the because, why, or even labelling your cruelty and evil. Fish does not say, '*You eagle, you are evil*'. It does get eaten by the eagle. It is the vitamin and strength for the eagle's fleet; it is not wasted. Better than rotting away on the shore of a beach, isn't it?

Enjoy life as is, without any labels and without any judgments.

Judgement

Judgement has become a way of life – a way to live. It has become such an integral part of one's life that one can say 'No Life – No Judgement'. There is LIFE, so there is judgement.

Judgement, or the act of judgment, can be looked at from various point of views or ways. Judging in situations can lead to improvisations, to possibilities and to different ways of living life or different ways to look at life. Judgement means different possibilities to a situation.

Let's look at another situation. '*So, this is the way I am, this is me. Today, this is how I am. Want to judge me? Go ahead, it's your prerogative. Whether I accept your judgment or not, is my choice*'. So easy, isn't it? It's simple.

The one judging and the one being judged should let the act take place without any heaviness (heavy feeling) and without any strings attached to it, so one can understand different point of views and concepts. That's it. Do we all ever know how we will react to a particular situation? Not always. It all depends upon how our day is passing. So let's remove all the heaviness attached to judgements and let all the judgements just be judgements and that's it. So much will resolve for the world then, for the chain of judgement is never-ending. How many judgements will you accept, believe, and change yourself for? Whenever you do such a thing, one more judgement will be ready to welcome you.

So enjoy judgement too as a gift. Gift to know that there are more possibilities available, more ways of living available.

'I have more choices, so cool – life is fine. I can live my life the way I choose. Fine – this way or that...so many ways. But no matter what I choose, judgement will be waiting to welcome me with open doors. So, cool.'

49. Take the Side Lane

It is so simple. When life takes a U-turn, then one must find a way to take the next 'side lane or service lane' out, or else we will go back to the same life and the same situation. Take the side lane and go into the unknown alley. Go and find a way to escape the 'not again' situation. Find something else to do, some other thought or some other way. One has to deliberately find a path of escape by finding an alternative side lane.

The flow of energy needs to be distracted smoothly and unknowingly. How does one do that? By first distracting our self and expanding our thinking to acknowledge that there are more possibilities. Once our energy is smooth and calm, we will know that something else is positively possible. Always work on self first, then attend to the other one who needs help. That's because if the self is not fit and fine, then we all go to that U-turn lane together (back to that same situation).

When life takes a U-turn, find the next side lane out. Deliberately take an 'unknown alley' to escape the 'not again' situation. Use your imagination.

Imagination leads to the conception of an idea, which then leads to action and creation, does it not?

Vivid Imagination – Idea – Action/Creation

That's how it works and functions through vivid imagination. This process is not even deliberate, it is just how we are made and that's how we function. It is so simple. But what do we do? We imagine the worst, in order to be prepared and then create it, unknowingly. Then we claim, *'I knew it, I knew it'*. No, it is actually *'I created it. I created it'*.

For instance, the telephone, train, television and the Internet were first a part of someone's imagination, weren't they? So let's go ahead and create wealth, good health, happiness, success, just like that and in the same way

.

PAST

50. Isn't Your Past Significant?

Why is there so much significance to our past? Why can't one forget the past, especially those memories that reminds one of painful situations and move forward in life, as if the past did not happen at all?

Well, let's look at it this way: '2017' is actually a number. It is a representation of a year and all that happened in that year. That number has a treasure chest of experiences, emotions, sufferings, happiness and events attached to it.

If I take away the year 2017 from your reality, will those experiences leave you? Those emotions that you had experienced in that year, will they leave you? No. If I take away the year 2017, they will still exist, as you have evolved! Those experiences have made you what you are today. You are a full story, a full book in itself.

Every creative, imagined or so-called 'year' has space in your being, in your existence, in yourself, in making you what you are. If any one year is removed, you will be incomplete, isn't it? Something will be missing in you as a creation. In you being 'you', you cannot remove 2017 from you, as that is what has constructed the present you.

Is '2017' actual? It is just a number given. However, experiences and events that created 'you' are actual. We should be thankful and grateful for our past, as our past has created us. Where you are now, all your experiences, be it good, bad, right or wrong, are all what you are made of. And now, because of the past experiences, you know better about what to choose and what not to choose, in your present and in your future.

So how should one choose to live? We all say live in the now. Let's honestly face it, that it is not easy. Thanks to our past, we know what to choose now and how to live. But we all know that it is not very easy to forget the past.

How about accepting and acknowledging everything lightly? Try saying, *'Thank you past, and now I choose this. My future will be wow as that is my expectation.'* Disappointment means time for a change of track, path or road and choose something new and move on.

Giving undue weightage and importance to life creates so much mess. Let's just live by realising and enjoying the fact that now I know better and I can choose better. Yes, I made mistakes; well, who hasn't? And it's okay. I shouldn't be crucified for it. It is my learning experience, however, now I know better.

51. Drop That Guilt

Guilt is a very intense emotion. Although a huge and a vast concept, guilt can be visualised from various angles and places. Guilt is very necessary to enable an individual to make a choice that is lighter (feels lighter within) because the feeling of guilt is very disturbing.

Guilt will help you choose some other way next time. It is actually a stepping-stone to many other pathways. It helps one to look for more possibilities and choices. At such times you have to be grateful to this emotion for feeling the way that you do, because it pushes you to choose some other way.

Now sticking on to the feeling of guilt and making it one's drama for the rest of one's life is an individual's choice. No one is asking you to do that; that is completely up to the individual. It is baseless and not required. A feeling of guilt encourages and guides you to choose another route; whether you take it or not, that is your choice. One has no reason to stick by it and cry over it for the rest of one's life. You had made a choice, it was your prerogative. You took that prerogative and that's that. It will reap a result which is a result of the choice that you have made.

Guilt is a very tiny emotion or feeling that is hyped up unnecessarily. It just lets you know that that's not a path you must take next time. That's it. Feel it, and then drop it and move on. Guilt is nothing; it is an extension of a drama that is not required – a boring movie. Give it no space.

52. Keep Your Past in the Background

Well, let's start fresh and new. Can we? Is it a possibility? Yes, always.

We have the capability to start fresh and new as we have the ability to keep our past in the past. We have that in us, even though our body does remember.

How, you ask?

Well, because we are constructed that way. Our completion until now includes yesterday. However, we do have the ability and choice to keep the past in the background and move on. Isn't that an amazing ability? And you know what? We all have this ability, undoubtedly.

We all have a choice to move ahead,
look forward, enjoy now and keep the past behind.

This choice is available to all. That's how we live. So aren't we all amazing creations in ourselves? Are we all not absolutely amazing pieces of work? Are we not doing an amazing job with ourselves? Each and every human existing is doing that, irrespective of where the human comes from, his caste, creed, geographical placement or colour.

53. Make It Spectacular

Wow, it's wow time. How does one live a 'wow' life? By opening one's eyes wide and change the scepticism to spectacularism. Try and feel the energy of that word – *Spectacularism!*

Every time you feel that you are in a ditch, change it to a question – 'How can I make this spectacular?'

One has to snap off the judgements, snap off the guilt and regrets in life, flip to the other side of the coin and make it spectacular and flourishing.

BELIEVE AND TRUST

54. Magnificence from Here On

Last year was a year of magnificent acceptance of a bright and a colourful life. It is possible to realise the magic of a magnificent accepted life, you see.

So, what was 2018? It was a year of space, a window, an open doorway to a higher consciousness, to a space of magnificent gratitude, to a place of abundant abundance and to a changed world. Let's talk about this changed world. So we all have created and asked for a world of happiness, isn't it? We had sowed the seeds and it is time to reap the fruits. The year 2018 was a time to reap the fruits. It does not mean that you stop asking. You continue to ask, keep that on, but ask from a higher consciousness for that space, that wholeness and that likeness.

It is just a matter of time to accomplish it all. Yet, you would like to create more. So both your *ask* button and your *receiving* buttons should always be on. With your empty bucket and with the sweetness of believing, watch and enjoy. Yes, enjoy the happiness; that is all that you should do and be grateful for it all.

Bravo and contentment are the master words of enjoyment. You celebrate and appreciate and then you are contented. You celebrate and appreciate again and continue to move on in this manner.

The year 2018 was a year of peace and stability. Stable is your life too, so enjoy. It's very crucial for you to enjoy happiness with abundance receiving and it is equally important for you to be thankful.

So, in 2019, live in gratitude for being 'all that you are' and for existing 'in all that is'.

Continue welcoming the unknown this way in gratitude.

55. Can't Life Be About Love?

How about we make life about love?

Let's make it about love and not despair,
about love and not hurt,
about love and not hatred and killing.

Let's rejoice, correct ourselves and correct others too to check themselves while discussing hatred. Let us love beauty and life. See beauty in everything. Make life about love and beauty, for 'the beauty of love' is all that we are.

Pain is no gain,
calm, peace and love are.

Man wants prosperity, victory, moksha and nirvana, doesn't he? However, it is first important to be peaceful, calm and at ease. Slowly and in no hurry, consciously and mindfully move forward. Why worry so much? Let's just move ahead with love, with ease, grounded, slow pace and sleep well. Peace be within all of us.

What has happened to people today? Where is love lost? This was never taught. We need to bring love back. This is our purpose. Write and speak the language of love always. We need to understand love, for it is not difficult and then we would have conquered the world.

56. Evil Eye – Is There Such a Thing?

Who has created us? The Creator, the Source, God, whatever name you wish to use.

The point is that if you are in alignment and if the Creator has created you, how is it possible that another human's eye can affect your life?

How is it possible that someone who has less power than the Creator can affect your life just by looking at you? Are human beings that powerful? Even if they are that powerful, can they be more powerful than the Creator itself?

Can the creation be more powerful than the Creator?
If you are in alignment with the Creator,
under no circumstances can somebody's eye ruin anything
of yours, can it?

57. Doubt or Believe, The Choice Is Yours

The way we believe in doubt, the amount of dedication and energy that we give to doubt and to our fears, if we stick to our belief and give the same dedication and energy to our belief, how would it be then? Just imagine!

58. Are You a Believer?

When flowers bloom,
when water flows,
when birds chirp,
and when the wind blows
... all that is life.

This thing called life is so… it's so simple. When a sand storm blows, when it rains heavily, when the sun shines bright, do birds complain? Do the flowers complain? Does the water stop flowing? If it doesn't enjoy the flow, it evaporates and takes another form, doesn't it?

Why do we humans complain? Aren't we more gifted than birds, than flowers and the rivers? Can't we find our way out? We can! The only issue is that we as human beings call ourselves believers but we, in the true sense, are non-believers and the excuse is 'I am only human'. Does the bird say that 'I am only a bird?' Does the flower go, 'I am only a flower?' We humans, however, have complaints and excuses. Even though we are very strong, beyond anyone's imagination, yet we are not ready to go there.

It's time to become a true believer as nothing can uproot you. Like a bird that sleeps on a tree at night, irrespective of any storm, or strong wind blowing or rain, it stays put. Neither the storm, nor the rain, nor hail affects the bird; it does not fly out of the tree. It stays put and continues with its sleep at night and it knows that God will take care of it. During a storm, the trees and bushes sway back and forth, but the birds sleeping on them, stay put and do not fall down even when the branches sway. In the same way, a true believer remains aligned and unaffected during challenging times or a storm.

Are you a believer? Do you remain strong, unearthed and deep rooted within your belief when the wind blows hard, knowing that the storm shall pass, or do you just complain?

Trusting, Believing and then Knowing

Look at an infant – he trusts. He tries to walk, falls, gets up and walks, falls again but still continues to get up and walk. He knows that this journey of falling and getting up will lead to something awesome. It always does.

When you *believe*, you have to take it to a *knowing* level.

Belief is '*I believe that it has happened*' (even if it hasn't happened yet in your reality) and not '*I believe, but why has it not happened yet?*'

Know that once you believe, that's it. '*I believe, so it has to happen. That's it!*'

So it is not just a simple belief; it is a strong *knowing*! Take it to your knowing level!

Look at this example and it will become clearer to you. When you want a certain promotion, you are expected to first ensure that your actions, attitude and behaviour are already of that next level and warrant the promotion. This attracts the promotion. So you receive what you already are. Similarly, the law of attraction states that if you want happiness, be happy; if you want love, be love; if you want abundance, live in that feeling of abundance by being grateful for all that you have. Be first what you desire, and it will be yours.

59. Aren't We the Chosen Ones?

It is so difficult for us as human beings to believe in ourselves. We live in doubt. No matter how much we are rewarded and how many times we are successful, all it takes is a tiny needle's prick to destroy our confidence in ourselves. And then we embark on a journey to find ourselves. But hello! Where are you going? What are you looking for? Look inwards. Ask yourself and have confidence in the answers that you receive from within you.

You are so blessed to be alive in this reality; you are the chosen one to be gifted this body; you can see, touch, taste, feel, breathe, imagine, dream, create goals and succeed. If you fail, you learn and bounce back up again. You can move on, you can forget the past and you can create a happy future.

You can drive, you can create cars to drive; you can build buildings, you can imagine and then build your imagination into a home, give home to them all.

So hey! Where are you going and what are you looking for? It's all in you! You are magnificent, an exclusive creation of the exclusive Creator. What else is possible for you; with so much talent in you, what more do you need to keep your confidence in yourself intact? What are you cribbing about? Who are you judging?

If you remain with the confidence that you are built with and believe that all will always turn out for your benefit, and you know that a beautiful thing called death is the worst that can happen, life for you will be so easy that a game of cards will seem more complicated. By the way, you have created that too. Confidence in you, is in you – *is you*!

60. Believe

For a change to occur, change is required by you, by believing. Until you actually believe, you will continue to go through drama.

We must concentrate, care enough and believe that the final destination is the Source or the Creator. Laughingly say, *'I will enjoy the journey – no matter what'*. Laughter changes the energy all around, doesn't it?

Laugh, no matter what.
Walk with belief and move continuously
till the final destination to eternity,
knowing that nothing can touch you.

You can change everything with your mind, with thoughts, with love and with passion. Fear is fine too as long as you can spring out of it.

61. Believe It. Leave It.
It Will Happen

A wise soul once had said to me, *"So when I was young, energetic and successful, I was sad regarding a situation that I was in. Deliberate happiness is all that it took, to take me out of my sadness! Believe it, then see it…"*

'*Happiness is all it took, to take me out of sadness*'. Sometimes, that's all it takes.

Dr Wayne W. Dyer had explained it best in one of his talks. "Look at a dark room whose door is closed with no trace of light inside. Once you open the door, the light from outside immediately enters the room. It does not say, '*Wait! I will slowly enter bit by bit*' or '*oh! The room is so filled with darkness that there is no room for light to enter*'. It just enters the room, instantly!"

So is the case with happiness; if you choose to open that door and allow yourself to be happy, happiness almost instantly enters you. Open all the doors and windows of that dark room within you and let the light shine in from everywhere and light up your room instantly.

It is a continuous and conscious awareness that we bring about at every moment of our lives, where we do things and think things that give us peace within and happiness. So let us smile, think happy thoughts, be conscious of our choices, choose what makes us feel light and happy in the moment and not heavy and uneasy within.

Let us create happiness deliberately.
Allow our feelings and knowing to guide us.

It is like the placebo effect. If you believe that it is happening, it is happening! So let's stop worrying and start believing. One does not have to make a conscious effort to believe, just put the thought out there and let it be.

Only when one believes that something is possible,
will one allow it to become possible.
Once you believe it, leave it.

Do not dwell on it too much as it will happen. It has to! One can steer and create one's own life in this manner, no matter what circumstances life brings forth in our path.

So let's start believing!

62. What Is Destiny?

Our choices depend upon our beliefs and our beliefs are often consequences of our choices. It can be both ways, you see. It's up to you, whichever way you choose. We have to understand that the outcome of our lives will depend upon what we believe and what we believe is where we stand.

Now, for instance, twins are born in the same house, more or less in the same environment and same experience, yet they turn out to be different when they grow up. Why? It's because their life turns out to be according to where they stand, what they are all about, their beliefs, their experiences, the choices that they make, how they take life individually, and as per their excitement. Their choices depend upon what excites them, you see. So they turn out to be different.

So, life can be any which way. It all depends upon where you stand. Of course, your experiences do count, but so does your grasping power. All work together hand in hand.

It doesn't always have to be one way only, it can be multiple ways, working together at the same time. You perceive life as one, because you are visualising it from one space. There are many more ways that you are unaware of and that you call possibilities, isn't it?

63. Self-Doubt

People have trust issues with self and hence they have problems when receiving. They can trust others such as parents and friends, but they doubt themselves. Isn't it? So how is that helping? How is that helping you to create your desires and to bring it to fruition?

Self-doubt has to be removed. It is not needed and not required. Your self will take you to the journey beyond your desires.

Just move, know, trust, believe and move in the knowing.

Self-doubt, self-sabotage, self-pity, unworthiness of self leads to failure. Change all that to self-assurance, self-confidence and self-worthiness.

Believe in self and then watch the reality change to awesomeness. Just like you wanted it to be and more.

64. Stay Calm During a Storm

A ship can only survive a storm if it is strong in its core. If the storm is stronger, the ship, no matter how strong, will sink. So how do we keep the ship on its path if the storm is strong? The key is to believe and trust. These will sail the boat till its conclusion. Doubt will wriggle the boat and fear will make it sink. Trust and belief will create miracles and magic. So we need to be calm and wait for the storm to pass.

The storm might pass the ship, or the ship might pass the storm. You see, no storm is permanent; it dies down. One just needs to be patient. I know, it is easier said than done, but let's try and do it, shall we? Let's try to see how it feels when we are amidst a storm.

Let us experiment. Next time when you are in the middle of a crisis, try to stay calm. Calm every molecule and cell of your body. Breathe in and out calmly. Be aware of the fact that you are deliberately doing it. Then manage others involved such as your family members. Just as on a plane, the instruction is to put on your oxygen mask first, similarly, calm yourself first and then attend to other members of the family. Try it!

Turbulence

So, how much do you believe?

When a turbulence comes, what is the first thing that one does? Wait for it to leave? Do you leave the plane? Do you panic and say *'oh my god! Why is this turbulence here?'* No, you peacefully sit in the plane, listen to the instructions of the pilot and wait for it to leave. Once gone, you unlock your seat belt and then go walking again, come back and sit. So why can't you do that with life?

The body is the plane and you are in it. You face turbulence and it takes you up and down. You wear your belt till it leaves you. Then you continue your journey, simple. It's really that simple.

But some turbulences take the plane down, you say? Yes, true they do because it's time for the next journey then, that's why. Why to fear it?

Then you think, but some people survive and have bad memory of the incident. Yes, some people do survive because they are the hero and challengers of life. They still want more, they still want to enjoy the essence of life and want to set an example for the rest. They have a mission, a purpose. If there is no purpose, then there is no need to survive. The one who survives automatically becomes a hero.

65. Be That Flower

When a flower sees a mountain crumbling down, it stays put, unaffected by the falling debris. This mere flower stays there with its roots firmly stuck to the ground as it watches the mountain crumble. The flower continuous to retain its full glory and exude its fragrance.

Should the mountain debris have fallen on the flower, and if its petals had scattered all over the place, each petal would still have retained its fragrance and beauty for as long as it is was possible.

Anyhow, when this flower, still intact and stuck to its roots, is spotted by the people who come to investigate the crumbled mountain, they get distracted momentarily by its beauty. Even if it is just for a few seconds, it does bring a smile on their faces, a delight to their being.

Prayer in the middle of a challenging situation is like that. During an unwanted situation, a prayer will uplift, just as the flower does for the onlookers on a crumbled mountain and a disturbed surrounding.

HAPPINESS

66. Change the Mood

Feeling low and down at times is okay and fine, as that's part of living. When you are feeling this way and want it to end, hope and imagine the up-phase and how rewarding it might be when you choose it.

Let's not completely ignore the possibility of low phases in our lives, for these do come; we just need to be aware of them. These are just temporary phases and will always be followed by high phases.

> Give yourself a time limit to be sad.
> Then once you cross your time limit,
> become a deliberate creator of happiness.

And how can you do that?

By listening to music, by movement, by watching stand-up comedies and funny shows. It's simple. Repercussions of a bad mood can be distinct and defined and so a change of mood is very important. Try it!

67. Deliberately Change Every Situation to a Happy One

What do you wish that life should offer to you or to us human beings (in general)?

Happiness, wealth, abundance, good health, comfort, peace, relaxation and so much more? That is possible. All you have to do is set your mind to it, that regardless of any circumstance, *'I am going to concentrate on happiness, success and well-being. Anything else can just happen as it wishes, but I am not going to be a part of it'.*

Yes, it is very difficult for human beings to live like that, but this time and era requires it. It requires human beings to concentrate on the fun aspect of life, to be able to take earth to that space and place. Earth has and is going through a phase of deep, deep evolution, so are we, and so is the universe. We all are interconnected. What you go through so does the earth, the universe, and the entire Oneness.

So it's clear that you are never alone in whatever experience you are having in life. In order to change it all for you and for the entire Oneness, be aware of your thinking and your experiences. Try to change every situation to a happy one.

Happiness is the key to all abundance, wealth and good health and celebration is the way to it. Laughter changes energy. So what will proving yourself right gift you?

Laughter will change your cells, will change your presence, your universe and expand and evolve it all and more. Don't we all want the earth and the universe to head towards happiness and evolve rather than towards sadness? It is time for every individual to be a contribution towards happiness. The messages of happiness all around us is not just in vain, it is a base for change.

Don't you think that the universe has gone through enough trauma and disturbances? It is time to change its energy and all that lies in our hands, each one of us. We need to concentrate on being happy, on laughter, on jokes and comedies. The era of stand-up comedians, why do you think it has come up? Because it is a requirement.

Laughter is the essence of life.

Laughter encourages love and happiness

Laughter cures

Laughter brings change

Laughter brings out the best in you and others

Please laugh, laugh at everything…Live in joy!

Make this year a deliberate year of laughter and laugh as much as you can as you go along. Laughter changes everything, it can cure everything, it can, and it will! At every possible time and at every situation, laugh and see for yourself. It instantly changes one's energy and others' too.

So choose laughter and joke about every aspect. Yes, it may not be easy initially, but make it easy, the rest will be taken care of and easily managed.

Be happy and laugh, no matter what! Being in the space of laughter, life will get easier, simpler and easily accessible. Let's all enjoy our time on earth.

Live in Joy

If you want to live your life, then live your life, or else what is the point of coming here?

Take small risks, live a little, otherwise what is the point of having this human body?

People are tired of the boring, mundane life, so how is this called living? Make people realise, have fun, otherwise what's the benefit of life and living here?

If you say that there is so much of grief in this world, how can one have fun always? Well, there is happiness too. That's why celebrate and have fun because everything is an illusion. There is zero and there is infinite too. So chill! Nothing serious is going on here. Distract for a bit and then things will change.

Switch Off!

Let's switch off our minds. Do it in action. Press the off button of our minds and listen to some foot tapping music. Let's smile and move to it deliberately. But the minute we are aware of our train of thought, let's immediately press the off button. Or better yet, pull the strings off, the connection, the connecting wire to those thoughts. Remove them, cut them, unplug them, dismantle them, because it is not needed.

To create a new and better world, we don't need to go out and march. We need to work at self first, then our extended family and friends and then move on. If one person also chooses this way of living, the mission is accomplished.

68. Laughter Is the New Way Out. How Is Being Sad Serving You?

The fun stuff is easy to get. It is indeed very easy, but one just has to want it, be it and desire it. It's not so difficult and no so hard. It is, in fact, light and easy. There is no reason to stress over any situation. Relax, chill and distract yourself by doing fun stuff. Doing fun stuff is the easiest thing to do.

Look, the drama will go on because that's how people get attention. No one will pay attention to you if you don't create drama. It's simple logic. It is the desire of attention that creates drama, importance, fulfilment, unworthiness and going to any extent to show that '*I am here even if it means sickness, drama or tragedy*'. Would anyone pay attention to Cassias Clay changing his name to Muhammad Ali unless he had a story attached to him? Would you notice or care if anyone was inspired by a comedian? No, you would say, 'so what'? But if that was a person who has come out of a struggle? Then yes, it would be inspirational for you. A comedian making you laugh so loud would make you say, 'Hah! Crazy guy!'

The entire understanding and the concept has to change. Get inspired by people who make you laugh, not cry.

Happiness is so easy and simple. Laugh – dedicate some time every day of your life to laughter. Laugh at something or watch something funny every day and see how you can change yourself and the world.

Laugh and you will become beautiful.
Laugh and you will become happy.
Laugh and all your desires and more will come to you.

It's simple you see, this venture, this adventure called life and its journey. It takes you to ups and down, achievements, success and happiness. Actually, it is always more of that because that's how you are created – through a feeling of exhilaration. That means that life should also be lived like that in order to create more in life.

Yes, life also gives sadness and heartfelt pain, but it has also taught us the tool to bring ourselves to that happy, exhilarating state again. There is a tool to come out of it all because happiness, success and exhilaration are inevitable and are more on earth and universe.

Again, look at all that the humans have created. Come on! Look at all the buildings, cars, parks, television, telephone, planes, should I go on and on? No way can a sad, depressed human create all this.

So in order to stay happy, make yourself happy deliberately; watch comedy shows every day as it keeps one in a happy place. It keeps you focusing there, you see. Enjoy life, be happy and you will change your life.

BREATHE. YOU ARE NEVER ALONE

69. Focus Leads to Clarity

Life is all about happenings, you see. The nuisance i.e. the annoyance, the trouble, is not in the being, it is in the happening. However, happenings can be cleared, they can be reduced and dealt with.

How? By focusing. Clearing our mind and clearing our heads and by keeping our focus.

Do you know how candle meditation works? In candle meditation, one is required to focus on the flame, focus on the light and then the darkness surrounding the light disappears. One is expected to look at the flame and stay in focus. The glowing light given out by the candle actually removes the darkness for the onlooker who focuses.

Similarly, focus eliminates all that is not required
so that our mind can stay clear.
It leads to clarity.

70. Breathe in Your Healing

If one says that 'life is a piece of shit', what do you think one will receive? Shit, won't they? Let us explain. In one lifetime, an individual comprises of flesh, blood, air, fire, heat, dust, wind, sand, metal, minerals, soul and magnetism and also the past, present and future. A human is a combination of everything that is available in the earth individually. Everything visible or non-visible in this existence is what a human is made of. Isn't it?

So how come a bit of imbalance or lack can create such an imbalance in the body that a human being falls ill? That imbalance can be corrected by just asking that particular aspect of earth's substance to just merge with your body. You can just ask or just touch (as the skin is an organ that absorbs) that particular aspect of earth, and just breathe it in, and just absorb its existence, its energy by just being in the same vicinity.

Well, whatever you feel you lack, breathe it in. Be aware of it, imagine the concerned lack and just breathe it in. So you see, this life is no piece of shit. Just ask the universe to heal you every day and it will. You are made of it. Every aspect of life, everywhere you experience lack, just ask it to change to abundance by asking it and this earth, this universe and this existence will give it to you. It's the only way. Do you get it? Just like that, it will happen. No drama is required. Only asking and believing is required. Life is so simple if you see it. Think about it and try it.

Breathe.
Breathe and connect.
You can connect to anything and everything.
Breathe and connect.

Breath is the connecting wire to anything. It actually connects you to your desires, your aspirations, your healers and yourself.

Breathing slow and steady will connect you to what is,
what ought to be
and what will be.
Just breathe.

This is so amazing as the breath takes you as high as the sky and beyond imagination. It also takes you to your base, and *woosh* takes you right up to where you wish to be. It may even take you where you cannot imagine to be.

Pay attention to your breath, give it a lot of importance. It's so significant, this breath. It will serve you well. It will connect you to your blocks and will clear them away with dignity.

71. Are You Ever Alone?

Is this life as we know it? Is it really?

Let's analyse now, shall we? Life – what is LIFE?

Living irrespectively for eternity – is that what it is?

Life as we see it, is body! Wow!

Having a body – Oh my! Touching, feeling, tasting, seeing, learning, laughing and jumping! Experiencing life without a body? With the body, with matter, the experience is wow.

And the body is our pet to take care of. It is our accompanying friend and we are never alone. The body is always with us doing exactly as we desire, listening to everything we say and feel.

Yet we abuse it. Yet we take care of it last. We give significance to money and wealth more rather than our body that has been with us through thick and thin, don't we? Let's enjoy our bodies and take care of them. The body actually has the capacity and potential to create more bodies, so let's nurture it, savour it, love it and compliment it. It is in our hands.

You Are Never Alone

Also, being alone is never the case. No one is ever alone, you see. When we are in this reality, there are days when we feel alone and lonely. But if we know any better, no one is ever alone. It is just a myth and reason for self-pity.

How can one exist alone? It is not possible. Oneness will never leave you alone, because you are part of it, isn't it?

72. Your Body Is a Gift

Gifts do not always necessarily have to be material bound, however, in this reality, most of the time they are. So our body can be as materialistic as can be. How can anything else be a bigger and a huger gift? Yet we humans harm the body first, neglect the body first and abuse the body first, not realising what would life be without this body?

Now let's examine. Is there a life without your body? Can you experience anything without a body? Can you experience money if you don't have a body? Can one experience success if one does not have a body? Then who has given us the right to abuse the most precious gift of life? Okay, let's presume that you are one unhappy soul. Everything is going wrong and nothing is going your way, and you say that you have no reason to live in this world. Correction.

The gift of life is the reason to live.
The gift of this body is the reason to live.

Feed it, nurture it and take care of it.

Life is as beautiful as snow. Exposure to harsh circumstances will melt it, unfavourable climate will melt it, but will it be destroyed? No. It will turn into a river and flow. It will flow with ease and then join the amazing sea and eventually evolve and join into the ocean. You see, snow is not spared too. It changes its existence and appearance to a larger experience. It evaporates, still it eventually does come down as rain and snow and so on and so forth.

So do we. We change, keep on evolving and having experiences like the molecules of water in snow, rain, river, sea and the ocean. But our body is the only thing that helps us to experience this material world.

73. Your Hands

During a new year, it is a great time as people are very happy, and they look forward to a great year ahead. Well, it's nice when people are happy, as the energy flow is amazing. Happiness actually truly expands right out through your hands into the atmosphere.

Hands are… wow! What can just one part of your body do? Do we realise? Gratitude to these pair of hands, for all that it does.

It creates,
it supports,
it helps,
it beats,
it asks you to stay silent,
it thanks,
it wails,
it welcomes,
it rejoices,
it holds your heart when you require,
it wipes your tears,
it keeps your arms warm…

It's your hands that do so much for you and you experience all that and more as a whole. It's a part of you. You experience it while it does your work, don't you?

That's what you are for that God, that Oneness. If you don't create, how will he experience it all? If your hands stay in one position, are they of much use to you? Think about it.

74. The Mighty Mind.
Use It, Not Fear It

Mind is an amazing gift. People need to use it for its benefits rather than fear. Mind is so magical and powerful. Come on, do we need to be reminded of what all man has created with the mind? The iPad, the pen that you write with, spectacles, The Burj Khalifa – the tallest building on earth – the Internet...? Oh, the list is endless.

Human mind is the best gift ever.
Let's use it and not fear it.
Let's use it to enhance ourselves.
Use it to create success for ourselves and others.
Let's use it for creating magical lives for ourselves.
And why not?
We can do so by believing,
by going to that 'I don't know' space
and then, voilà, creating fantasy.
That's the way; in fact, that's the best way.
So how amazing a life will you be creating for yourself?

75. Dreams Wash Out Our Fears and Emotions

The body is a marvellous gift. After a good night's sleep, each morning it is filled with new energy. The dream state is a journey of cleansing where all the points of view that are stuck in your body and in your energy are cleansed.

Nightmares

Nightmares are fears within us, that come out in the form of dreams. For instance, when you dream predicting a natural calamity, sometimes it is just that you become aware of what is going to happen somewhere on earth. This can happen because you are tuned in and thus are aware as a being, and by having such a dream, you are able to clear that information out.

You see, somewhere the cells know that something is about to happen. This is because you are made of this earth and somewhere this earth is becoming aware and sending your body the information, that 'this' is what is happening.

A dream is like every cell and molecule in your body is taking a shower. You physically take a shower and wash off the dirt, but how will you wash out the emotions and the feelings and the fears within? That is done through dreams. Dreams happen when you are sleeping; repairing happens when you are sleeping. The grease gets out, and you polish the whole body once again to a pure and more functional form. So when you are dreaming, the body is just repairing itself, and what is not required is thrown out in the form of a dream.

76. Be a Contribution

Mountains, the moon, road, pathways, the stars, they all have gone through perhaps more in life and living than you have gone through. But you are too busy living your own life. Have you ever thought about their story? Has anyone ever asked the universe what it wants? They all are a contribution to us and our lives. What about us being a contribution to them and their existence? Have we ever thought about how we can be a contribution to them? Think about this.

You can just see your so-called 'miseries'. But the moon and the stars are witness to it all. The moon does not say that I am not coming out today because I can't take it anymore or I want to run away or destroy myself. It continues to shine its light on us and this reality.

There must be more of the 'wow' factor than sadness,
to allow the moon to choose to shine every night
or the sun to glow every morning.
The earth must be worth it
for life as we know it to exist in our lovely planet.

77. Listen to the Silence

Listen! Listen to the silence!

Has anyone tried to listen to the silence? Do you know how much of activity takes place and how much of noise there is in that silence?

The frequency of that silence is not matching your frequency, that's why you cannot hear anything. Once you start listening to the atmosphere or the space of the silence, voilà! You'd know that you have reached the next level of evolving.

Let's try this exercise, shall we?

Sit in silence and make a note of all that you can hear.

It takes you to the space of infinity. In that space is where everything exists. It's where decisions are made by Oneness, where birth and death take place. That space is where exchange happens, new stars are constantly forming, planets are moving and there is so much of activity taking place. In that silence you will realise that it is a space of peace.

So much is going on there, but we are unaware of more than half of such activities. Why? Because our frequency has not reached there yet. Those levels and connections have not happened. Silence takes one there, to those levels, and whenever in this reality you feel too much is happening, just become aware of that space of silence and how peaceful it is, despite of so much movement. Despite of all the activities, bring that peace into this reality – bring beyond the beyond into this reality.

SMALL SIMPLE

78. Life Is Simple

In this era, whatever you imagine you will get, you will become. Life is precious, and you realise it now, at this stage.

It's time to reap your soul.
It's time to understand life.

And it's time to sit back and relax and say, *'Been there, done all that, now what did I learn?'*

You see, life is beautiful and becomes more so now after you marvel on your achievements. You get life's worth now. You couldn't possibly get it before because you were busy living it before. Now you are so busy analysing it. Well, that's how life moves, expands and moves to another level of possibility.

It's simple really, don't make it so intense. Every bacterium, virus, cat, dog, mosquito, human being, are existences in different forms. All do everything in their power to secure their home, community and their existence. Human beings create war, even declare war on humans itself. Why? Don't we want others' living existence too? Not wanting others' existence – how is that possible? Even they are creations by the Master Creator. So who then will win the battle of life?

The one who is aligned with Oneness; the one who knows that it is just a board game and that all will be fine eventually; the one who pulls out of fear; the one who resonates with 'I don't know' and with the unknown; the one that believes that there has to be more possibilities and the one who choses another possibility, and by not doing destruction (*vinaash*) of another existence.

I don't know to the unknown to other possibilities.
It is simple. Life as we know it, is simple.

79. What Is Power?

The power of life is simple, yet so powerful. We often associate power with heavy energy. Power means strong, tough and hard. Really, does it really? Is that power? No. Power is simplicity; it is easy going and it is a light energy. Power is a smile.

A small child can win one over with one simple light look and a smile. That is power. That is strength. That is easy going. For that smile, one gets ready to give a child one's whole world. That's the power that the child has over you. So who says power is strength, toughness and hardness? Power is so simple, so easy, so light that one's presence itself is enough to win a party over.

So let's make a conscious effort to be powerful by being simple, with a smile on our faces. Let's endeavour to consciously smile all the time and remind each other to smile. Let's carry it on our faces all the time. Soon the smile will penetrate into you and the body will smile. Once your body smiles, then the environment around you will also smile. And then you become powerful. Get it? It's so simple.

80. Spread Compassion

The planet needs compassion, companionship, tender touch and loving care and so do people.

How about starting from home? How can one create a change in the world if they cannot manage their own home?

Small Steps

Let's start by loving our home, members of our immediate family, then extended family, then neighbours, friends and so on... small steps.

81. Baby Steps

So, the basis of living is to take baby steps as you move. Take baby steps, enjoying every step, like a baby does. For every step that a little baby takes while learning how to walk for the first time, how do we react? We jump, we clap, and we rejoice at every step, don't we?

So why don't we do the same for every step that we take, or every new choice that we make for each new journey? Imagine the energy of everything that we will change then.

You want the new generation not to be depressed? Then let's do that. Let's encourage them, clap for them, for every step that they take. They might fall – babies do, you know – but they will eventually learn how to walk.

82. Simple Is the New Mantra

Life as you see it, is not so very complicated. Each one of us has to trust ourselves.

First have confidence in you. It's all about self-confidence. Choose the answer or the way that feels light, easy and simple.

Solutions always lie in simplicity.

The way to live your life lightly is to choose simple solutions, choose the simple and the light way.

No, it's not finding the easy way out. Life is about living on easy paths. Why would you want to live a difficult path?

83. Make It Small

How can life, as we know it or don't know it, be fun?

No matter what the circumstances are, you just need to mould a situation to your lovable, likable path. Life can be less complicated and more relaxed if you eliminate the disturbing factors from it.

How does one mould, you ask? How does a sculptor mould the clay and discard the unwanted parts? The same way.

How do we mould if the unwanted parts are in your face all the time? Well, it's so simple and easy… make it small. Small. Just imagine that you are in space, looking back at earth. See how small will he or she or that look from up there? It is not even visible from up there. You are no one if seen from that big a picture of reality and space. Earth is only a dot. So imagine what he or she or that is.

It is so easy. We have the power to make someone or
something huge and big or tiny and inconspicuous.
Use your power. Simple.

84. How Are Complications Serving You? Keep It Simple.

It is very simple and clear that life should be clear-cut, crisp and plain. Keep things simple and clear. Run and move away from complications and complex people. Is it needed? Is it required?

Life as we know it, creates a lot of ups and downs. Doesn't it? But what if it is our expectation of ups and downs that is taking us to our ups and downs?

Let's start at the very beginning. The way we want it and the way we wish it should be.

Back to Simplicity

It's so simple, doesn't have to be so complicated and it doesn't need to be so messed up. It doesn't have to be an amazing equation created by another human and rest of the world trying to judge the capabilities based on that human's equation. No!

Life can be simple as the birds chirping and the beautiful sounds of waterfall. It can be as simple and as sweet as you sitting on a swing in a garden and enjoying the gentle breeze hitting your body and face as you sway back and forth. Where has all that simplicity gone and vanished? Bring the people to basics. You will not need to go for a retreat; start going to the park every day. Watch children play. That will be as good as meditation.

Keep It Simple

Life as we know it and feel it, is simple. There are options and choices to choose from. Let's make it simple and choose simple things. Let's ask what would be simple to choose? What will help me lead a simple life and how will this come to me in a simple manner? Now is the time for simplicity. All answers and solutions will come to you in a simple manner. Instead of looking for complications, look for simple solutions.

It is all about keeping it simple.
Complications aren't working anymore.

Let's go to the simple solutions, simple habitat and simple way of living. Simple way of life will give so much more space to people that the reason for drama will change. Be simple. Avoid assumptions. Know that it's all going to be simple. Solutions are simple. This is the era of simplicity. That's why people are downsizing.

Simplify and Move On

The level of our understanding has become better. Now we are ready for the next level. So it is still simple and easy now that we have clarity.

Simplicity can take one to places, really, truly. Things become easy if we perceive them to be easy, before they happen. Take a situation out of its complex journey by first declaring it to be easy. More than half of the battle is won then, once you declare a situation to be easy. The rest of the situation that follows just falls into place.

Before you come across any situation or before planning,
declare it to be easy, exciting, fun and then move.

Things become easy if first, we in our mind, perceive it as being easy. So take 'a situation' out of its complex journey (no matter how complex it may seem), see its simplicity and it will be easy to handle. The other elements which complicate it further will automatically be taken care of, similar to the domino effect, once you focus on the simplest aspect.

Declare a situation to be easy, simple, exciting and fun to solve and then move on. If a situation has multiple complexities, then break them down into simple parts and then move on with ease.

Life is simple. Look for simplicity, simple ways to handle a situation. Ask every time…

'How can I handle this situation in a simple manner?'

Ask every time when you are in a pickle…

'What is the best and simple way to solve this?' That's it!

CHOICES

85. Choices

So, life can be lived in three ways:

- Keep moving on without thinking or analysing and facing consequences according to our choices.
- Thinking, analysing and then making choices. Holding ourselves accountable for our chosen actions and the results thereafter.
- Choosing to live our lives according to others' perceptions, their point of views and their experiences. Making others' experiences, ours.

Which way is a better way to live? Any which way. All are experiences. One can live in all the three ways, how and when he likes. One just needs to be aware of the conclusions or by-products of the choices that one makes.

The journey of living a life that is filled with gratitude, adventure, curiosity, completion, satisfaction, achievement, etc. is a marvellous journey. It is not as evasive as one presumes life to be; in fact, it is subtle and creative. A journey to create for self in a simple manner or creatively rough manner, an easy passage or a hard passage, it is all up to us, what we choose under the given circumstances.

So what is the best way to complete this journey or episode called life? Should it be interesting or funny? Should it be sorrowful or pitiful? Should it be of a hero or a challenger? It all depends upon the choices that we make.

Yes, sometimes we are not aware of the choices that we make. Most of the time we are unaware whether our choice is good or bad, right or wrong, or we just trust our instinct and make a choice. These choices take us to various rooms of a house. These are various rooms of life where every room stands for something. So you, your choices and the room that you have chosen, together create an experience called your life, that's all.

Sometimes we learn from the experience and sometimes we just move on, that's all. How you play the game in that room or live your movie in that cinema, all depends upon you. Now you don't need to crucify yourself for your choices because that's the best you thought you knew.

86. Consequences

Life is all about making choices. It's one's prerogative. I consciously choose to do this or that and I am ready to face the consequences that come with it as a result of the choices I that make.

Consequence is such a huge word. Why is this word taken as a negative word? A consequence can be positive, you know. It can be just right.

Why, you ask? Because *I chose it*. It is right for me now, this very minute, as I choose it. That's all!

What will be the consequence of my action? Well, it will be just right and perfect for me. It will be what is required for my wellbeing. No further questions and discussions, thank you. We human beings need to live this way. Well, at least try. Life will be less complicated, wouldn't it?

87. Commitments

Now, this is a new space of acceptance.

Let's say that you have made a commitment. Then later in life, you get a peak of a dream – a dream that you have never ever experienced before, and your desire is to experience it now. But what about your commitment? What do you do? You had made a commitment in life and now how can you change your commitment?

You are forgetting that you too evolve and change, that's inevitable (*Niyam*).

Note, many commitments have created wars, jealousy and pain in the past. Commitment and promises do not work anymore. The truth now is…I evolve, I do, and I have evolved. I can make a commitment and then realise that the commitment is not serving me anymore, it is of no contribution to me and thus I will change my commitment to you, so I can experience something else that I desire because this life is also my life.

If you have a right to fulfil your desire by asking me to commit, then I do have the right to live my desires by choosing to back off now.

You see, the era has changed, and the people have changed. It's okay to realise that I want 'something else' now. If it didn't go as per your plan, 'oh well, at least one tried'. Desires and dreams evolve constantly as you evolve. It's okay to relax and change your perspective towards commitments.

Let Go of the Chains

Relationships on earth are all about emotions and commitment, oaths and promises; even marriages are based on that. Promise to be by your side – till death do us apart. But what if my desire to create something for myself is not in sync with you now? I am not going to wait till death do us part, am I?

This life is so obliviously crucial to create more and more. Abundance is what we all talk about, but we do not want to leave the place that is chaining us down. We need to understand that in order to live life to the fullest, we have to let go – let go of the chains that are stopping us from moving ahead. If you give significance to the chain that is stopping you or limiting you, you will not be able to progress. In order to progress, we need to make the chain invisible, feel light and be free from the commitment to move ahead. You can surely keep the relationship, however, remove all the chains that are barring your relationship – be free and then move ahead.

How can one be free? Well, breathe the chains out. Imagine the chains disintegrating and coming out through your breath. Make them feel light and lighter within you (in your mind) and see the magic in action.

I am sure that you are thinking that this way anyone can enter and exit a commitment easily and that's not fair to others. Also, where is the element of trust then?

Life is but a game. Isn't life all about the choices that we make and their consequences? Doesn't one know that he is responsible and accountable for the choices that he makes when he enters into a commitment? He is not oblivious to the fact that there is a possibility that either party may opt out. He is also aware of the consequences that may arise when he either sticks to his commitment or drops out of it, happily or unhappily.

So when two parties are entering into a commitment and if one person knowingly chooses to alter his commitment, then he and the affected party must be ready to face whatever consequences that may arise as a result of their choices. Surely both parties were aware of all risks involved before entering into the commitment. Man is accountable and responsible for all his choices and the consequences that result from it, isn't he?

88. You Don't Have to Struggle to Be a Hero

It's so simple and easy to live this amazingly gifted life in an easy and effective way. But life has become a struggle for a lot of people and that has been placed now as a standard towards accomplishment in this reality. It has become the norm to overcome a struggle, then to be identified as a winner and that is supposed to lead to success and a happier life.

One struggles, then gets victory over the struggle and is declared a hero. And why not? You are a hero if you overcome your struggles and circumstances. But the point here is, why is struggling and overcoming a struggle the only criteria for becoming a hero? Can't one become a hero without a struggle?

Who is a hero? The one who is successful? The one who overcomes unwanted and unattractive circumstances? But there are individuals who have 'become something' in life too without any struggle, who have it all, and had it all from the very beginning and who remain happy most of the time in their journey of life. Do you see 'them' as heroes? How many of these heroes have been written about?

That's because to maintain yourself at the top is also not easy; hence, these are heroes too and must be acknowledged.

In this reality, some people say…

'Oh! You had it all from the very beginning and thus life was easy for you.'

'Oh! You did not struggle at all in life, so sorry you don't fall into the category of a hero.'

Really? How about saying …

'Wow, you had made the right choices for yourself. Let's analyse how you did it.' Or:

'Sure, you were born with a silver spoon in your mouth, but you were the one who knew what choices to make then, for your success today.'

I think it is time to acknowledge even those people who make the right choices for themselves in order to be successful and happy, who didn't need to struggle. We should make them an example for their society to analyse, so that others can also learn and move ahead, choose ahead and make further improved choices. Life can be beautiful, amazing, happy and successful without struggles, you know.

It's time not to give so much significance to struggles, but to give more weightage to possibilities by making choices and then moving further.